Know and Be Known

Know and Be Known

Small Groups That Nourish and Connect

Brooke B. Collison

THE ALBAN INSTITUTE

Herndon, Virginia

www.alban.org

The Alban Institute
2121 Cooperative Way, Suite 100
Herndon, VA 20171

Scripture quotations, unless otherwise noted, are from the New
Revised Standard Version of the Bible, © 1989, Division of Chris-
tian Education of the National Council of Churches of Christ in
the United States of America, and are used by permission.

Library of Congress Cataloging-in-Publication Data

Collison, Brooke B.
  Know and be known : small groups that nourish and connect /
Brooke B. Collison.
    p. cm.
  ISBN 978-1-56699-335-7
  1. Church group work. 2. Small groups--Religious aspects--
Christianity. I. Title.

  BV652.2.C65 2007
  253'.7--dc22

                                        2006103115

    11   10   09   08   07   UG   1   2   3   4   5

I dedicate this book to my family—
the most interesting small group I know.

◉ Contents

◉ Foreword

The journey of faith that has brought me into the office of a bishop of the United Methodist Church began with a small church in a rural setting. Drawn into the activities of that faith community by members and friends who loved Jesus Christ and the church, I was invited to be a part of many groups. Sunday School classes, the choir, confirmation class, youth group, and a circle of persons who gathered on mornings before school to share about our faith journeys were just some of those groups I participated in.

As I reflect on these experiences, I have a deep appreciation for the relationships that were formed because of these groups. Each offered vital connections that at times served as a lifeline to God, to the faith, and to others.

In those days churches were growing as a natural consequence of the demographics of the period. It appeared that one could simply build a church, open its doors, and the pews would be filled with the worshiping faithful and Sunday School classes would be bursting at the seams. Such ease at populating churches gave Christians a sense of calm about church growth and development. And somewhere along the journey since then many churches lost either their ability to provide for the spiritual needs of the members of the church and the community or the churches, more tragically, ceased to care.

More recently, as the options for church attendance and spiritual growth and personal fulfillment have increased in variety and as we have become increasingly more secular in our orientation, churches find themselves scrambling for survival. Energy and resources are easily focused on such mundane matters as raising adequate funds to cover the annual budget (including escalating costs for salaries and benefits); costs to maintain aging facilities; expenses of ministries, mission and programs; and costs related to denominational askings. Spiritual needs of the members and the community may be in danger of neglect.

For those who long to shift the focus from the corporal to the spiritual needs of the congregation and the community, small group ministry is one tool. This ministry is a means by which the spiritual needs of a congregation may be met through the connections that are developed, strengthened, and nurtured through participation in small groups. My experience has demonstrated that these groups offer opportunities to increase the quality of the spiritual experience in our churches. In *Know and Be Known,* Brooke Collison offers a theological foundation for small groups in churches and presents detailed, step-by-step practical information to help form such a ministry.

The human need for and yearning for connection and belonging are addressed by small groups. Newcomers are often attracted to churches by worship opportunities. We might walk in the doors of a church on a Sunday morning in order to experience the preaching of a dynamic pastor or to hear the moving chords of organ, piano, or guitar. Some may be drawn by programs that pique a visitor's interest, such as children's programs, youth activities, or ministries of social justice. Whatever draws persons to the church often brings them to the sanctuary or other worship space for praise and prayer. At the same time, many need to be fed spiritually in ways other than what can be provided by a worship experience.

In such situations, Collison offers the small group as a potential answer to this need. While he warns readers that "a small group ministry is not a panacea for all problems," he nonetheless suggests that such a program is a "vehicle to address some issues and conditions missing in most congregations." Clearly, there is no easy "one size fits all" package. Starting a small group ministry requires dedicated efforts by faithful leaders who are willing to invest time and energy and active participants who are willing to make a commitment to make things work. Yet at the same time a small group ministry can begin with just a few interested persons, and thus all churches might well benefit from the guidance and encouragement Collison offers.

Collison's practical work offers a detailed and coherent methodology for the formation of a small group ministry. Once established, it is imperative that such a program also be nurtured. Some of the commonly experienced situations that are addressed by Collison include handling confidences, dealing with conflict within the small group, and how to generate ideas for discussion.

And, ultimately, those who participate in the program must be open to the movement of God's Spirit, which requires flexibility and openness to change. There is a natural "ebb and flow" to small groups that presents challenges that must be addressed. As in any human endeavor, members of a small group may not get along well. There may be conflict or disagreement or times when individuals do not participate or when one person monopolizes the conversation. Collison addresses these and other dynamics of small groups from his own experience as a professional counselor and as a leader in his local church settings.

And finally, Collison explains that while in some cases small group ministries may endure over many years, in other cases they may need to change or even cease to exist. Even these long-lasting small groups may be in danger of settling into a static mode and may lose the impact or excitement or meaning that spawned their existence. This resource offers insight and direction to keep small group ministries vital in order to respond to the needs of the participants and to honor the changes in attitudes or interest of those who belong to the small groups.

While we cannot offer instant, easy answers to the dilemma of how to connect people in an organization as varied and complex as a church, we know that small groups are one viable answer that has brought about dramatic change and vitality to some churches. Small group ministries can make a difference. As I reflect on my own faith journey, that small United Methodist Church that loved me and nurtured me in my relationship with Jesus Christ did so by inviting me to be a part of several small but dynamic and formative small groups. They were a part of my growing understanding of what it meant to be a part of the body of Christ. And I am hopeful that as you read and utilize this resource you will find vitality in your faith journey as well.

Robert T. Hoshibata
Resident Bishop
Oregon-Idaho Annual Conference
The United Methodist Church

◉ Preface

Sixteen years ago, my spouse and I were invited to join a small group. We had moved to a new community because of my job. My spouse was feeling uprooted, torn away from her friends, positions of responsibility, status in the community, sense of a life purpose—the list could go on. I stepped into a position where I had status (senior rank at a university), responsibilities, an instant colleague group, and something to do. I had changed location; she had changed her life. We did have one common and continuing element in our new home—life in a church. Although the congregation was new to us, the denomination was familiar; thus, hymns and rituals fit like old shoes. In addition, we had visited the church once before and had received the church newsletter for five months before our move, so we knew names, programs, schedules, and the like.

Two couples in the church, also new to the community, invited four other couples to meet for a six-week "trial period" as a *koinonia,* or fellowship, group. With great reluctance, I consented to attend six weekly sessions, all the while thinking I didn't want another scheduled responsibility. I also didn't think I "needed" a group, because I had been through a variety of group processes as a faculty member in a counseling program and had previously been in a men's group that met weekly for several years. I agreed to attend because I knew my spouse needed some connections and personal relationships. I decided I could endure a six-week trial, but a small group certainly wasn't something I either needed or wanted at the time.

Sixteen years later, the small group still meets weekly for two hours, and we recently completed a two-day retreat where we reflected and evaluated where we have been, where we are now, and where we want to go. A lot of what I have put in this book comes from my sixteen years' experience as a member of the small group. The rest comes from other group experiences, observation of groups, and teaching about groups in counselor education for 30 years.

This book will promote development of a small group in your congregation, including suggestions about how to get started, how to be a member of a group, how leaders can help groups function, and how to work with some of the most common issues that arise in small groups. Finally, I will share some of the life of the small group that has nourished me for the past 16 years.

I would like to thank several people for helping me get my ideas about groups into words, sentences, paragraphs, and, eventually, this book. At the outset, I thank Joan, my spouse, who said to me when I retired, "I hope you'll write a book." This may not be the one she had in mind, but she has encouraged me every step of the way. I must also thank Janet, Jim, Bill, and Ellen for extending the invitation to join a group for "just six weeks" sixteen years ago. Thanks also to the other members of the group: Rick and Debbie, Doug and Linda, and Jim and Joyce for putting up with my continual questions during the writing. I owe a lot to my former students, who always taught me more than I taught them. And any technical knowledge about groups has come from some great faculty colleagues—Reese, Jim, Liz, Judy, and Mary Lou.

I extend a huge thanks to Beth Gaede, my editor, who read every draft, revised, suggested, questioned, encouraged, challenged, and read again. She forced me to become a better writer, and our electronic dialogue has indeed been a pleasant creative experience.

Thanks, in advance, to those who will read this book. I hope it provides something for you and the groups you will lead or be part of. If, as you read, you have suggestions, ideas, or comments, feel free to pass them along. To contact me, visit the Web page for this book at www.alban.org.

BBC
October 2006

Chapter 1

◉ Why Small Groups?

For many people, the word *church* conjures up an image of people assembled in a sanctuary on a Sunday morning to worship, sing, listen to a sermon, and perhaps exchange a few hasty greetings or brief conversations amid tight clusters of folks who all seem to know each other. Some churchgoers approach the Sunday gathering hoping they won't have to interact with others in a "meet-and-greet" time. A few may stand alone, silently hoping someone will notice them and reach out to make personal contact. Others seem to relish the noisy, incomplete, elbow-to-elbow communications that take place with coffee cup in hand.

It's almost as if two worlds exist. In one, the people who know each other exchange quick greetings in a stand-up gathering of acquaintances. In the other, isolated folk slip in and out of the church, not necessarily by choice—perhaps without saying anything other than "thank you" to the official greeter who handed them a bulletin at the door. Each world may be satisfactory for some, but not all. Both worlds lack a key ingredient—the extended interaction that permits people to know one another with depth or substance. In those brief conversations I may tell another what I have been doing, what trip I have been on, what fish I caught, or what I plan for the week ahead, but I don't say much about who I am inside.

For many people, brief interactions are not enough. They yearn for human contact and the sense of belonging that a small group can provide. People in our modern electronic world of e-mails, voice mails, blogs, and depersonalized messaging hunger for real human relationships. That hunger can be nourished through the face-to-face, quality interactions that take place in small groups. When we feed others, we are similarly fed. When we are fed, we thrive. And when we thrive, the church is filled with life. Small groups thus nourish churches just as they sustain the parishioners who meet together.

This book is intended for church leaders who want to initiate a small group program and for members of small groups who want to learn about effective small-group dynamics. The rationale for developing a small group program in a church is simple. In a small group, people can know others and be known in ways they cannot in large groups. In small groups, they are able to connect—to find the nourishment essential for life. This connection lies at the heart of the small group, a gathering that provides members of a congregation the opportunity to be part of a close, caring, supportive community. The first two chapters of *Know and Be Known* are intended for planners of the congregation's small group program. Later chapters provide information useful to small group members, leaders, and planners of the small group program.

Why Another Group?

As important as small groups can be for people, the question "Who wants to join a small group?" typically won't get many "I do" answers when first asked. More people are likely to respond "Not me" than "Yes, me," especially if the proposed group is a support group that might go on for a long time. Churches have a hard enough time getting people to sign up for a short-term task group, let alone for a group of people who may not know each other but who are expected to sit together and share their life stories. So who wants a group? One answer: "No one."

However, many people want what a small group can provide. Planning can begin with a few church members who are familiar with the congregation and understand the purpose of small groups. It is important that they begin their discussion with questions such as why initiate a small group program? Or, why another small group? Planners will create a firmer foundation for their work if they then focus on even deeper questions:

- What personal and interpersonal needs are not being met by our current structure?
- To what extent do people feel isolated, alone, unconnected from others?
- When we examine the nature and structure of the groups that currently exist, what seems to be missing?

The group may want to frame the same questions positively: What personal and interpersonal needs are being met by our current structure? To what extent do people feel connected and known? A planning group can also develop its own questions, such as how many members of the congregation know three or more people well? Valuable sources of planning data may already exist—annual reports, consultant studies, clergy opinions, recommendations from congregational studies, ideas generated in study groups, and so forth.

A small group program may not work in every congregation. It may not be the answer to the issues present in your congregation. But a small group program can provide the opportunities to connect which many people yearn for. Why another small group or a small group program? Your planning team might conclude that a small group could provide a place for people to develop connections. Or a small group could reduce the sense of isolation and loneliness that some people are feeling. Or small groups could provide a place for people to work on spiritual formation (if that has been defined as "something missing").

Because every congregation is unique, I do not offer a universal set of conditions or reasons for creating a small group; I recommend that your congregation develop its own list as you understand congregational needs. From my experience, however, I suggest the list might include the following:

A small group provides a place where

- people connect,
- friendships and supportive relationships grow deeper,
- members support one another in crisis,
- people accomplish tasks and service projects,
- people have fun and enjoy each other,
- members study topics and have in-depth discussions,
- members explore and enrich their spirituality,
- participants are personally accountable to friends.

Based on what your planning group knows about the people in your congregation, your list could be much different from the one above. The best list is the one that describes the needs to be met by the small groups you will organize. As groups are formed and begin to function, they can continue to develop and refine their own lists of needs and statement of purpose. An ongoing small group is like any living organism in that it changes with time and circumstance. Even though studies of church groups often reveal near-heroic efforts to avoid change over time ("We have always done it this way!"), I urge small groups to schedule intentional time to review what they are about in order to do more than simply maintain the status quo. What will you do as a group to grow, serve, and remain a vital group? What the members of a group want or need from their group in its early development may be far different from what they want or need as the group matures.

In addition to creating an awareness of what the small group can provide, be mindful, as planning teams and members of small groups, of other ways needs are met in a congregation.

A small group program is not a panacea for all problems. It is a vehicle to address some issues and conditions missing in most congregations. If you develop a small group program that lets some people connect with others for discussion and mutual support, the congregation also needs to respond to those who are not members of a small group. Creation of several small groups that develop a sense of identity and belonging among the members may leave others in the congregation feeling as isolated as before. In your planning, considering their needs is essential.

What about Other Groups?

Some people's needs are already being met by organizations that are not part of a formal small group program—but that are indeed small groups. Small groups go by many names: covenant group, study group, companion group, and the like. These groups have one thing in common: the size is usually limited to between eight and twelve people. Social scientists who study group behavior often talk about the number 12 as a limiter for effective and efficient groups. We know the number worked for Jesus.

Every church, large or small, has many groups: choirs, trustee groups, study groups, classes, financial campaign task forces, social response teams, potluck gatherings, critical care committees, and on and on. Why would a church so full of groups need another way to get people together? Because most groups in our churches and throughout our culture begin with the task or activity in mind. The relationships follow—if participants are lucky. But many church groups focus on learning, praying, or serving others within or outside the congregation rather than on addressing the hunger for deep relationships so common in contemporary society and today's church.

Of course, people who gather to learn, pray, or serve can form important connections in those groups. Choirs organize to sing, but the choir members may value the friendships among members as much as (or more than) the rehearsal or performance aspects. Study groups organize around the topic selected. Still, although members learn, they may value the relationships more than they value the lesson. And when the topic or book has been completed, the study group members may continue with another topic because they don't want to lose the connections with the people. (An article in my local paper recently described the 50-year anniversary of a book group, quoting one member as saying that they had remained together as good friends by making certain they didn't review books!)

Ideally, however, small group programs in churches put the relationships first and the tasks or achievements second, intentionally addressing the nurturing aspect of small groups. The members may develop numerous tasks or activities over time, but the relationships remain as the essential core component. Whether a small group is established to work on a task—a service project, an educational objective, or spiritual growth—the common element emphasized in this book is the reason for forming another small group: the relational or support dimension of the group's life. How the members interact with each other and the personal bonds they develop will be the glue that holds the group together over time.

Yes, support groups can include tasks and projects in their activities, and task groups can attend to the interpersonal dimensions of the members. The interpersonal support aspects of all groups in a church are important, however, even if the groups are formed for some specific task or function. Service groups, education classes, book groups, Bible study groups, worship groups, and spiritual renewal groups may be organized for a specific purpose that doesn't include interpersonal support. But addressing the support dimension of the group's function is important, just as focusing on the group's primary purpose is important. Service, learning, and spiritual growth are essential to healthy group life; however, the interpersonal support is the glue that holds the group together through all its other work. The interpersonal component is also challenging for most groups and often receives the least attention.

I urge all church groups to attend to the interpersonal needs of members. Accomplishing tasks may be the primary focus of task groups, but giving attention to how the members are connected, what their concerns are, and how their lives are progressing is also essential—in the same way that service, learning, and spiritual growth are essential reasons for the existence of interpersonal support groups. Whether the group is a task or support group, both the task and the interpersonal components must come together if either goal is to be met in full; otherwise, the groups are only a fraction of what they can fully be. The connection, support, comfort, and belonging that develop among a group of people who meet regularly are what ultimately make it possible for the group to perform its chosen task.

The next chapter continues with the process of forming groups. If your planning group has decided that a program of small groups is a good idea, how do you get the groups started? Chapters explaining the skills needed to be a member of a group and how to be a leader follow.

Chapter 2

◎ Launching Your Small Group Program

Your planning group has decided it would be great to create some small support groups in your church—so what do you do next? Just post an announcement on a bulletin board and say, "Groups will start next Tuesday"? Sorry. It doesn't happen that way.

We know how task groups begin. Someone, perhaps the chair of a governing body, appoints a group to undertake a specific task and gives them a start and a finish date, and the group begins its work. Some task groups may be defined by the governance rules or bylaws of a church, with the membership and range of responsibility clearly defined. Such groups might take care of church finance, manage church properties, plan worship, oversee personnel matters, and the like. Education groups often start and end according to an established calendar of classes. Teachers are named and people sign up for a particular class or children and youth in a specific age group know they are to go to a designated classroom. Interest groups frequently begin at the urging of one or two people who identify a topic or activity—quilting, softball, or some issue, such as environmental concerns. A meeting time and place is announced, and off they go. A group of people who have similar situations in life—such as new mothers, people with a common medical diagnosis, or people going through a divorce—may begin with referrals from a clergyperson or some other group in the church that watches out for individuals with personal concerns or needs. Small groups designed for interpersonal support seldom get started the way task, learning, or growth groups do, however.

It may sound obvious, but a small group program should start small. Churches that want to initiate a small group program need to plan, recruit, train, and support the program to ensure success. Biting off too big a chunk at the beginning will most likely result in the feelings of exasperation that doom too many program activities in churches and social service organizations.

Often, a task group is created for initiating a small group program. The group will want to consider questions such as these:

- How do you assist people who want to start a group?
- How are people invited or selected to be in a small group?
- Who would lead the groups?
- What resources are needed to help small groups function well?

These questions are just starting points for planners to expand on.

Developing an Invitational Culture

Ultimately, invitation is the key to creating small support groups. When an invitational culture permeates a church, people are more likely to be connected—to belong. Think what it would be like if every person—whether long-time member or visitor—felt invited to be a part of church groups. And consider how that experience would differ from a place where it takes extra effort just to squeeze your way in. An invitation to join a small group is a good way to make people feel welcome.

Who offers this invitation? The answer is simple: "Anyone." How nice to hear, "We want you to join a small group" or "A new small group is forming and we would like you to join us to see if it will meet your needs."

As I suggested in chapter 1, small groups thrive when they meet the needs of the members. People bring different needs to their participation in a small group, and the mix of needs results in every group being different; however, there are some pervasive human needs and characteristics every group can work to meet. So, what are the needs frequently associated with an effective small group?

- belonging
- having a sense of place
- fun
- learning
- accomplishing tasks
- providing support to others
- getting support from others
- personal growth
- friendships

Once a group forms, it will continue to meet a changing mix of needs as the group matures.

Even when people would benefit from a support group, they are not likely to announce that they are looking for a small group of people with whom they can develop long-term interpersonal relationships. People joining a small group will more likely need to be found and asked than they will seek out and find a small group. Announcements, sign-up sheets, bulletin inserts, or any of the other forms churches use to distribute information are not likely to catch more than a few people willing to start or join a small group. That brings us back to the invitation.

I recently asked the 11 other people in the small group I attend why they came to the first meeting nearly 16 years ago. All of them talked about the invitation they had received from one of the two founding couples. When I asked how many of them came to the first meeting reluctantly, about half raised a hand. None of them would have put their name on a sign-up sheet indicating they were interested or willing to join a small group. So why did the group get started? And more important, why has it continued for 16 years? The reasons:

The invitation was personal and direct.
The projected schedule asked for a six-week commitment.
The option to leave after six weeks was genuine.
The initial purpose was clear.
The leaders were effective.
The first six weeks of lessons and activities were interesting to group members.
The participants discovered something of value for themselves.

As well as that initial invitation worked 16 years ago, I offer this cautionary note about invitational groups: the danger or problem with inviting people to join groups is that someone may not get invited! As the church initiates its small group program, intentional inclusiveness is essential. People should be able to say, "No," but no one should be denied the opportunity to say, "Yes."

Your planning group, therefore, has a difficult choice to make—either develop a small group program so extensive that every person can be invited to join or develop a smaller start-up plan while clearly communicating that, as the program gets established, other people will have the opportunity to become participants. Be careful to avoid creating a start-up small group program that becomes or even appears to be elite, exclusionary, or selective.

Based on what your planning group knows and understands about your congregation, it can best determine how the initial invitations to join a group are most effectively made. The planning group may decide to invite people by neighborhood groupings, their age, identification as new members, marital status, or some indication of interest determined by a survey or questionnaire. Creating the lists of potential members offers

a church the opportunity to develop multigenerational and heterogeneous groups that reflect the community demographics.

Your planning group, using the knowledge it has about
your church, will design an effective system of inviting people
to become members of a small group. The invitations will be
made in a variety of ways and the groups will be organized to
meet the presumed needs of persons in the congregation. The
planning group also knows that effective groups need good
leadership—whether it comes from within the group or from
outside, leadership is a key ingredient for the start-up of a small
group program.

Leading Small Groups

The issue of leadership is as complex as the way
groups form and how they function. Key questions for planners of a small group program include these:

- Who will be the leaders?
- What leadership characteristics, skills, and abilities are
  needed?
- Can the skills and abilities be learned?
- How will the leaders function?
- How are the leaders supported once they begin their
  work with small groups?

As you assess the make-up of the groups you are creating—
their similarities and differences, as well as their needs—
consider the questions about leaders above and review them
periodically.

Some planning team members may advocate leaderless
groups—that is, creating the groups and letting them do their
own facilitation. Some people prefer that groups have facilita-
tors rather than leaders because they see the roles differently:
the implication is that a facilitator helps a group go where
they want to go, while a leader takes a group where the leader
decides. The group may want to consider other names or titles

to place on this person—convener, guide, steward, shepherd, and the like. My contention is that even leaderless groups have leaders, however. They emerge at different times.

Leadership is related to power and, in all but the most mature groups, potential struggles with leadership (in other words, with power) may disrupt the group from reaching its goals. Power is the ability to influence a group of people to do something. Power can be exercised by rewarding or punishing behaviors. Charismatic people who attract others who just want to be near them have power over their followers. Power may be given to a person who has extensive expertise in an area of interest for the group. For example, if the group is discussing health issues, physicians likely have power by virtue of the knowledge they possess. Power problems occur in groups when the leader wants the group to go one way and the group wants to go another. Of course, this describes a group where the leader is not trying to help the group do what it wants; it is a group where the leader is looking for followers. Power is not bad unless it is used for ends that are not constructive.

Who Makes the Best Leader?

Chief among the requirements to be a good group leader is the person's willingness and ability to put the group and its members first and herself second. Being a leader of a small group is not a license to tell people how to get their lives together, who to vote for, or what the right answer is to every one of life's many dilemmas. Being a group leader doesn't give you a platform for your own passion. The leader is there to help the group function effectively.

Being a leader of a small group does not require an advanced degree in psychology, counseling, or group process, but it does require attention to some basic skills. Effective group leaders do the following:

- Attend to the physical arrangements for the group (if another person in the group hasn't taken on the responsibility). Arrange chairs so people can see, hear, and talk with each other.

- Avoid making assumptions about the members of the group—how well they do or don't know each other, what attitude they bring to the group, or how they feel about being there.
- Listen more than they talk.
- Are attentive to how each person in the group appears to be doing at any given time.
- Help the group stay on topic, but are sensitive to topics that may be more critical for either a person in the group or the group as a whole.
- Help new groups stay within their personal comfort levels on topics, allowing people to grow in their sense of comfort and security with one another. Refrain from pushing the group into areas people are not ready to handle.
- Monitor the group for signs of conflict or confrontation that may disrupt the progress of the group.

The best way to develop a cadre of leaders is by invitation. The planning group may find that people invited to be leaders of small groups will respond with reluctance rather than enthusiasm. Planners are likely to hear "Who, me?" "You want me to do what?" or even "No way! I can't do that!" While acknowledging that leading a small group is a challenging role, the planning group also assures those invited to lead that they will receive training and ongoing support for their important role. Of course, the planning group needs to follow through and develop a good leadership training program and a system of continuing support!

How Can Leaders Be Trained?

A good facilitator for a leadership training program will model the style you hope your leaders will use as they work with members of the small groups being formed.

An effective training program helps potential leaders learn to:

- Tend to physical arrangements for the group—comfortable seating, minimal distractions, an environment conducive to discussion among the members.
- Be inclusive. Make certain everyone is greeted, introduced, welcomed. Watch for people who seem different or "out of sorts" from one meeting to the next as an indication they may have something in their life that needs attention.
- Begin with topics that are neither threatening nor embarrassing, and move toward the more crucial personal topics as the group matures.
- Invite rather than force participation, and include the option to "pass."
- Monitor time and find ways to bring discussions to a close without offending participants. Use strategies that move the group from the topic of the moment to the next session in a constructive manner.
- Help the group reflect on how they function as a group and how they can revise their own group goals.
- Reflect on and find ways to obtain constructive and honest feedback about their functioning as a leader (not to be confused with collecting praise for their leadership).

Organize leader training in a way that uses the knowledge and experience of the participants as a starting point. Are the recruited leaders old hands at the task or will they be leading a group for the first time? Be sure to address participants' individual and collective concerns about leading small groups. Training could also include discussion and role-plays of situations common to small groups. Some of those situations are described in chapter 6, "What to Do About . . . ?"

A more complete outline for leader training is included in appendix C. The goal of leader training is to improve the probability that the small groups formed in your congregation will nourish and sustain the members who participate. The goal is not to perfect leaders; it is to help groups function well.

How Do Leaders Function?

Group leaders can be internal to the group. That is, they can be group members who function in a leadership role. Groups can select their own leaders, and it is possible that groups can rotate the leadership function among members; however, all the members need to have the requisite skills to do this, and they must be willing to take on the leadership role at designated times. Key to this style of leadership is the willingness of group members to accept a different person as leader from meeting to meeting.

Internal leaders are members of the group first and leaders second; therefore, they need to be clear with the other group members about which role they are in. This is particularly true when the leader role changes from one meeting to another—a possibility, for example, if the meeting place changes as different members host and it is customary for the host to be the leader. You know who the leader is in advance because of the meeting location. Another way to handle changing leadership is for the leader to preface comments and remarks with statements such as, "As the group leader tonight, I ask you all to . . . ." A leader might also reduce her participation in the discussion whenever she is in the leader role.

Leaders can also be external—outsiders who are not truly members of the group. If a group is made up of people who don't believe they have the skills to be a leader, then it is logical to begin the group with an external leader. That person might facilitate the group's work during the initial stages of their formation and clearly indicate she will serve as leader only until the group reaches the point where members can assume leadership—either shared among members or designating one or two members to lead for a period of time. External leaders might work with a group for a specified number of sessions (time limited) or to accomplish a particular project (task specific). For example, an external leader might serve a group as a consultant or an observer to assist them with some issue or problem.

The external leader's functioning will change, depending on his role and how long he has been working with a group. External leaders may be very active during the early stages of the group. As the group continues to meet, the leader becomes less and less involved in what the group does and how it functions, so that at the time of his scheduled departure, the group has acquired the skills to handle their own processes. The model is much like that of parenting, where one goal of the parent is to have the child become independent. In the early stages of the group, the external leader might

- select topics,
- instruct members about how groups function,
- monitor conversations,
- attend to the affect or emotional tone of comments,
- mediate conflicts,
- give feedback to members and to the group as a whole on how they are doing.

In the latter stages of the group, members would begin to take over those functions. The leader might know he has reached the leadership goal if he fails to show up some day and the group functions as well (or better) with the leader absent. On the other hand, the group members may see the external leader as "expert" in some way for a long time. The leader may want to openly shift leadership responsibilities to members if they try to hang on to the person's leadership longer than necessary.

Consultant to the group is another external role. In this situation, someone comes to the group, perhaps from time to time, to help the group understand how it is functioning. The consultant may meet with the group for a designated period to observe and provide feedback to the group to help them understand how they are functioning as a group—what is working well and what is getting in the way of deepening relationships. The role of consultant, sometimes called a process observer, is delicate. As outsiders, consultants see what happens in groups through different eyes than the members'. As outsiders, their comments may or may not be welcomed—particularly if they are seen as critical of a person or an established process. For these reasons, consultants should couch their feedback in the form of observations rather than prescriptions: "I notice that as long as the food is available, there is little discussion of the topic," rather than, "You must put the food away and start on time."

Another philosophy of small groups says, "Every member is a leader." I discuss this approach in chapter 3, "How to Be a Good Group Member." What this means is that every member can utilize various leadership skills to ensure the goals of the group are reached. When members of a group are listening well, sticking to the issues under discussion, not providing more information than is necessary, respecting differences of opinion, dealing openly and honestly with strong emotion, and making certain that all members of the group are able to contribute, then the need for a designated leader is diminished. Leaderless groups are those in which all the members utilize effective group skills.

Leader Support

Just as members of a group need support and leadership in order to function effectively over time, leaders need the same. In an ideal situation, the leaders would gather from time to time to do their own processing. Without identifying specific people in a group, they could discuss situations they have faced in their small group—their feelings about the way they handled something or the kind of feedback they received from group members. Leaders can also discuss their reflections on being a group leader. Leaders primarily need a place where they can be themselves, reflect with colleagues on their own role as leader, and receive feedback and support.

Leaders also need a source for group materials. In appendix A of this book are suggestions for discussion topics for beginning groups, more experienced groups, and mature groups. The differences among the three developmental levels of groups are subjective. Experience isn't just a matter of how long the group has been together, but more how the group is able to monitor itself, the extent to which group members care for each other, and how the group is able to deal with a crisis or conflict. Many resource materials for small groups can also be found through a selective search of Web material—searching with descriptors such as "small group ministry," "small group discussion," "support groups," or "discussion topics" will produce more suggestions than a group could work through in a lifetime. Web searching will require some discrimination in order to select appropriate materials.

Small groups made up of people invited and ready to begin conversation with effective leaders who have been trained and will be supported in their work offer exciting possibilities for a congregation. When people come together in a setting that allows them to know one another better, to deepen their sense of spirituality, and to engage in activities that support each other as well as the church and community, the effect will be noticeable in a congregation. It will be more difficult for an individual to stand in the midst of a group of worshipers on Sunday morning and still feel isolated and alone. People will be able to connect. The experience of invitation and connection could even become epidemic.

Chapter 3

◎ How to Be a Good Group Member

Being a member of a small group is easy. All you have to do is show up once in a while. Right? Wrong! Group membership is hard work, and it requires skills—skills that some people seem to possess naturally, others acquire with little effort, and some struggle to develop. As with other skills, group skills can be acquired through instruction, experience, practice, occasional testing, and continual refinement.

This chapter and the next are primarily intended for small group members. This chapter describes several basic skills that will help you be a good group member—and will also help the group function most effectively. Good small group members do the following:

- Listen
- Speak in the first person
- Demonstrate understanding of others
- Demonstrate that others are important
- Give members equal time
- Contribute to the group

Listening

Listening seems like the simplest of tasks. But often we don't listen as well as we could. A good group member focuses on what a person has to say. Just as important, because much communication is nonverbal, is the ability to observe and listen to other people and hear what they didn't say, so we understand both what they mean and how they feel about what they are discussing.

The skills that accompany listening are specific:

Giving attention to the speaker
Maintaining eye contact with the speaker
Not carrying on side conversations
Avoiding distractions
Not interrupting
Trying to understand both the meaning and the feelings or emotional tone of statements, and communicating understanding through accurate reflections. A good listener doesn't just say, "I understand."
Not diverting the focus from someone by topping the speaker's story with one that is worse (or better, or bigger, or the like).

Speaking in the First Person

You know yourself better than anyone else in the group. When you talk in the group, use first person—"I feel . . ." or "I think . . ." or "I wish . . ." If you are angry about something, don't spend time talking about what another person did. Instead, talk about how you are feeling about the anger-provoking incident. Above all, don't waste energy in your group by focusing on group members who are absent or people who aren't members of the group. If your concern involves another person or group, provide only the basic details about the individual or people outside the group in order for other group members to hear and understand you, then bring the emphasis back to you, not "the other."

For example, the statement "My boss gave me a poor per-formance evaluation today and I'm really upset about it" provides information about the trigger event (poor performance evaluation), the outside person involved (the boss), and the one person in the group who can talk about the issue (you—"I'm upset"). It does no good to spend 10 minutes explaining how performance evaluations are done, whether the boss has credentials or respect in the company, or the result of someone else's evaluation. The important issue for you and the group is contained in the phrase "I'm upset."

Similarly, if a group member is upset with a family member, going on at length about what that person does to upset them is not productive. "My kid has no respect for my car. He doesn't change the oil, fill the gas tank, or wash the car when it's dirty. He took a shop course, but didn't learn anything in there." These statements may describe the parent's point of view, but the missing elements are the speaker's thoughts and feelings. For example, "I'm really upset with my son's lack of respect for the car. I get mad every time he brings it back dirty or with the tank empty, and I holler at him, but it doesn't do any good."

These statements from a parental perspective provide the group with substance for discussion. Another parent might respond, "My teen upsets me regularly, and I find I'm also hollering more than I used to." This could lead to productive discussion, whereas the question "What shop class did he take?" is about details that don't matter and are unlikely to lead to helpful conversation.

Demonstrating Your Understanding

Most of us have had the experience of telling about a difficult or a joyous situation and having the listener respond, "I know exactly how you feel." The speaker's statement, although well intended, is offensive and inaccurate. No one knows exactly how you feel, especially if you have just described a crisis, a difficult situation, or even a moment of extreme elation about good news.

When someone in the group tells about her experience, you can demonstrate your understanding by reflecting her feeling or by telling her what you understand she has said. This is the time you can use second-person statements: "You must feel awful." "You look worried." "Your face really lights up when you talk about that."

As I explained above, you demonstrate your understanding by focusing on the speakers, hearing their words, reflecting what you hear them say to you, and not topping their story with your own. When a person says, "I feel terrible, I scratched the paint on our new car," you don't respond, "That's nothing, I dented two fenders and a door on ours."

Discounting or minimizing what a person says—even if you strongly disagree—is another unhelpful response. Disagreeing without being confrontational is possible. "I don't see it that way" is better than "You are wrong!" or "You don't know anything about the subject." You can understand and disagree at the same time by restating what the person has said and then stating your own position: "You are saying we should increase the church budget by 25 percent. I would like to raise it 50 percent." This sort of response lets the dialogue continue, whereas "That's a pitiful idea" will likely stop the discussion or start an unproductive argument.

A good way to practice demonstrating understanding is to have two people pair off in a simulated or actual conversation (or conflict). One person makes a statement. Before the other person can make a statement, he must paraphrase or restate the first speaker's point to the first person's satisfaction. Even with controversial topics, this process helps the speakers develop clarity and understanding and slows the argument rather than having it escalate to some explosive point (and it's a great technique to use with children who are standing toe to toe, red faced and yelling). For example, here's a dialogue between Jim and Rick:

Jim: "That was a terrible sermon Sunday."
Rick: "You don't like the preacher."

Jim: "No, I just didn't like the sermon."
Rick: "You didn't understand what was being said?"
Jim: "No, I just didn't like it."
Rick: "Oh, you understood the topic but didn't like it."
Jim: "Right."
Rick: "What didn't you like about the sermon?"

The illustration may be a little hokey, but it shows how a listener can add to a statement inappropriate interpretation the speaker did not intend. Before you can move on to the next point in your discussion (or argument), you must agree on the meaning of the first point. The result of this process is that conflicts move forward more slowly, but they move with understanding—with more light than heat rather than the other way around, as is the case with many arguments.

People Are Important

The most effective way to demonstrate to another person that she is important is to clearly show that you are interested in her and what she has to say. Giving respect is as simple as greeting another person instead of ignoring her when you enter a room. In the vernacular of youth, "dissing" (disrespecting) someone is a quick way to start a fight. With members of a small group, ignoring or always disagreeing with someone are forms of "dissing."

Another way to demonstrate that people are important is to show them that you remember things they have said or done. In a group discussion, suppose one person says to another, "Three weeks ago you suggested a great idea for a service project for our group. Would you describe it again?" What he has done is to demonstrate that the person is important to him by remembering the contribution, saying it was a good idea and asking that it be brought up again for consideration.

People can be minimized in group discussions if an idea promoted by one person is rejected, only to have the same idea enthusiastically accepted when a different person submits it later for discussion. This same topic is discussed later in the book (chapter 5) when the issue of sexism in groups is presented. A woman describes how she has experienced having her ideas ignored when the same idea submitted by a man has been accepted. Her interpretation: "I am not valued." Minimizing also happens when another person dismisses an idea as unimportant or insignificant. For example, if "I'm worried about this lump on my arm" receives a response of "That's silly, it just looks like a bruise," the first speaker has been minimized and her concern discounted. The response says that both she and her concerns are unimportant.

Equal Time

Small groups work best when the members feel they have had their share of time and attention. Equal time can be managed in a number of ways. The mechanical method is to use a timer: "OK, your seven minutes are up, so pack up your troubles for another week and let's move on." Obviously, there are problems with this approach—especially if it is administered in the manner illustrated (I hope no one would be so insensitive as to say that).

The best method for assuring equal time among participants is for the members of the group to monitor themselves and others and to voice their observations openly. "I've taken too long with this explanation; I would like to hear what others think" is an effective self-monitoring method. Or, as a member of the group, you can be aware of who has and who hasn't talked and say, "I'm aware that [name] hasn't had a chance to speak to this issue. I'd like to hear what [name] has to say." The group leader or a group member can use the invitational approach in group discussion, just as small groups themselves are created by invitation: "I invite [name] to share her/his thoughts on . . ." You can be direct: "Joan, what do you think about this?" In your group, be sure to build in an understanding that a person may pass but reserve the right to speak later. Expressing a sincere desire to hear what someone has to say increases the probability that a frequently silent member will speak.

Must the amount of time each person speaks be equal in every meeting? No—there are times when a person will come to the group with such a heavy need that conversation might focus on them the entire time. The group may have matured to the point that the person can comfortably come to the group and say, "I have an issue I need to bring to the group and there's no way I can do it quickly. Can I have [a number] minutes?" Members can also call the leader in advance and request time for an important personal issue they want to bring to the group. At an early point in the group's formation, members should discuss how they want to handle particular needs or requests for extra time.

If the group discovers that the same person uses a majority of the group time every session, members need to deal with this as a group. Small groups in churches are not therapy groups. If one individual is so needy as to require all the group's time, then it may be necessary to suggest the person seek professional help outside the group. On the other hand, a person may be in a high-need state for a short period, and the group may be very willing to give that extra care. That decision is a matter for the group to discuss.

Can I be silent if I want? Yes—many people process issues and information without talking; others seem only to process while they talk. One person may make snap decisions while another must silently chew on the options for what seems like an eternity. Hasty responders have their hand in the air before the teacher finishes the question; reflective responders sit and mull things over silently before speaking. Often, by the time they are ready to respond, the discussion has moved on to another topic. One kind of responder is not better than the other, but being aware of who talks and who doesn't is important for group members. Effective small groups accept different styles of processing information and decision making within the group. The challenge for the group is to find ways to ensure that each person talks as much as needed in order to feel heard and understood. The issue leads to another good discussion topic for the group: How do you process information? How do you make decisions? This is a topic which will often generate some heat (and light) between life partners as they discuss how they have made decisions which affect each other—buying cars, where to go on vacation, how much to spend on recreation, and the like.

Contributing to the Group

Can you be silent and be a member of a group? Perhaps, if the members of the group need someone who only listens. But how can they know that you hear and understand them if they only have your silence? And how can it be a group if only some of the members contribute? Can you be absent and contribute to the group? Not likely, other than to provide a topic for conversation about your absence.

Each member of the group needs to find some way to contribute to the group in a manner that feels good to the member and is valued by the other people in the group. We hear from the apostle Paul (1 Cor. 12:14–26) that we are one body with many parts. Each part (group member) is important and its differences are valuable. All group members need to view themselves as important to the group, and the group needs to value the unique contributions of its members.

The question for members is, what role do you play in the group's life? Are you the questioner? The prober? The initiator? The includer? The caretaker? The activities planner? If you examine the role(s) you play in the group, do you play dysfunctional roles as well as constructive roles? Are you the objector? The blocker? The topic changer? The cynic? Or are you the encourager? The mediator? The peacemaker?

One way that members can assess how they contribute to the group is to pointedly ask themselves the question, what do I bring to this group? More mature groups, where trust has been established, can ask the question in a group session: What does each of us bring to the group? The group exercise can be extended by having group members say to each other, "The thing you bring to the group is _____." This exercise can be written or an open dialogue. If written, members of the group can write something for every member, using one card per person. The cards can be signed or anonymous; however, if the group has much history together, even anonymous cards will be recognized. I urge signed cards. It can be a powerful experience to receive a set of cards—one from each group member—and then read the set of statements (either silently or aloud). Talking about the effect of receiving and reading the cards should provide the group with a lot of discussion material.

Typically, a group member will see another person in a way the person doesn't see himself or herself—for example, hearing someone say she sees you as a deep thinker when you don't see yourself as a deep thinker. What is it like to hear that statement? What do other people see that results in their comments? What if you can't accept their description?

More difficult to discuss is how you see yourself or other members as not contributing or as impeding conversation. Giving and receiving negative feedback is hard, even when people might be saying these things about themselves. Receiving negative feedback is especially hard when the negative behavior is not the way we see ourselves. Giving and receiving negative feedback requires a mature group that has established a high level of trust and commitment to each other and therefore can handle this kind of probing analysis of contribution to a group.

Similarly, hearing people make self-critical statements and discussing those openly and honestly is an important dynamic of small groups. A group discussion can be framed so that members begin by describing ways they believe they obstruct the group's progress or by identifying behaviors they exhibit that don't help the group move along. In such a situation, other members need to recognize that a typical way we respond to people making self-critical statements is to negate the statement. We do it in order to protect the other person. For example, "I think I talk too much in the group" may be met with responses such as, "Oh, no, my goodness, you don't talk too much." The more honest response might be, "There are times when you seem to go on longer than necessary." In so doing we affirm the person's self-analysis without being critical of the person.

As another example, suppose a member of your group seems to make a joke of everything and it actually bothers you. She says, "I try to lighten things up when they get serious" (a self-descriptive statement, not a self-critical statement). If you respond, "It's no bother," that doesn't help either of you. Being honest and saying "It does bother me" is better. You might even extend the discussion with a question: "How did you develop that response pattern?" Or you can provide an observation: "Your humor seems to come at serious moments that aren't very funny."

Rather than negating self-critical statements or avoiding self-descriptive statements, group members provide a more constructive response by asking what would be helpful to people who have made such statements about themselves. For example, in response to the person who said he talks too much, one might say, "How would you like us to respond to you when you are going on too long?" Or to the person who talked about using humor when you believe it is not always helpful, you might say, "What if you tried not being funny in the next serious discussion?" or "How do you think people react to the humor in those serious moments?" Both responses promote additional introspection and dialogue about ways we interact with people.

A good topic for discussion in your small group is to describe the signals that group members, spouses, partners, parents, or friends use with others to tell them they are being too talkative, inappropriate, or insensitive. That may lead to discussions of other signals people use when they are trying to get another person to do something without saying pointedly what it is they want to have done. A small group of people who know each other well also may be able to describe the nonverbal or verbal signals used by group members other than their partners and have an interesting discussion.

The small group I am in recently had a session about anger: what made us angry, how we showed anger, and what we did with our anger. At one point, a member said, "Spouses ought to describe what makes their partner angry and tell how they show it." What followed was a humorous session with spouses demonstrating the nonverbal signals that said their partner was angry. It was a good-natured session.

Group members who practice the skills described in this chapter will have productive sessions. They will be able to engage in dialogue that lets people go beyond the superficial exchanges that characterize much that passes for conversation, either one-on-one or in small groups. Other aspects of small group life that enable the group to be more than a collection of people who meet together will be described in the next chapter.

Chapter 4

◉ What Good Group Members Talk About

A productive group does more than get together and listen to each other—although that in itself is a great beginning. Members in groups that function effectively do the following:

- Work on issues, effects, and meanings, not details.
- Avoid authoritarian or dogmatic statements and personal criticism.
- Learn to deal openly and honestly with emotions—your own and those of others.
- Maintain confidences and do group work in the group.
- Review the group's goals periodically.
- Work on group improvement.
- Give attention to members who leave and new ones who join.

Issues, Effects, and Meanings

Small group discussions are most significant for the members when they can focus on issues, effects, and meanings instead of details. Think about people you know who, when asked even a simple question, give you an excessive amount of unessential information in the answer. Others may generalize so much that what you get is "bottom line" statements without enough detail to understand the issue. Conversations become rich not in the details of an event but in the issues the event stirs up, the effects of the event on the person, and the meaning the person takes away from the event. Group discussion is most productive when a person presents enough information (or detail) for you to understand the issues without abusing valuable discussion time with information the group doesn't need to have in order to move forward.

There are also times in a group discussion when you are presented with information that goes beyond your comfort level. As an example, a member of the group I am in recently talked about a medical procedure, which made a couple of other people in the group uncomfortable. Many subjects may trigger discomfort for individuals—frequently things that have their own unpleasant history for that person. Like the child who asks where babies come from and receives more information than he is prepared to hear, some of us, in such situations of information overload, use "TMI," contemporary slang for "too much information" to let the speaker know she has crossed a personal comfort line.

A different picture is presented for many parents of teens who ask, "How was school today?" and receive only a monosyllabic grunt in response. Those parents suffer from "too little information" for their comfort level. On the other hand, if they heard everything that did take place, they might also cry out, "TMI!"

So how do you strike a balance between not enough information or detail and too much? As a speaker in the group, keep in mind that your listeners need only enough information to set the stage for the issues, effects, and meanings. If you are talking about your family vacation, the TMI version of the story might be, "We left on Tuesday at 9:43 AM. We planned to leave at 9:00, but John couldn't find his swim fins because he left them in the garage behind some lumber I stacked there when I installed the new bathroom shelves—they're about four feet long and made out of finished plywood that I got at the new lumberyard over on Sixth Street. . . ." This story could go on for a long time and never get to the issue. You have probably had to endure similar TMI tales.

The questions for the teller and for the listeners are:

What is the issue here?
What is the effect of the story?
What meaning do you take away from the event?

If the storyteller had focused on these aspects of the vacation, the story might have been, "We got a late start on our vacation this week, and I really got angry with the family (the issue?). Starting late spoiled the trip for me (the effect?). And I realize that I have to find a way to let go of my need to control (the meaning?)."

As a member of a small group, you can help the group stay on issues, effects, and meanings by monitoring your own statements for TMI. In addition, you can help others avoid excessive detail with the kind of questions you ask. Don't seek detail. Do comment on and ask for the issues, effects, and meanings of the stories they tell.

To be successful with this part of the small group's conversation, you will need to suppress your own curiosity about the details of stories. We humans do have a curious, almost prurient need to know more than is necessary—sometimes to see if the situation is similar to our own experience. However, our desire for detail doesn't help the speaker, and it doesn't get to the meat of the story. The truly significant conversation includes only essential detail.

Authoritarian or Dogmatic Statements and Personal Criticism

People who tend to be silent in group conversations frequently carry painful memories stemming from classroom or group discussion experiences. They may be afraid to speak up, thinking they will be criticized, put down, or diminished by critical comments from others. People are quiet in group discussions for many other reasons, but, as a leader or a member of a small group, consider that every person comes to the group with prior experiences that shape how he or she responds, or doesn't. Every behavior has a reason.

Criticism damages the self unless you are a competitive person who enjoys a verbal challenge. Criticism can be warranted, useful, even welcome—if it is respectfully offered within a relationship of trust. Small groups are not about combative verbal exchanges.

In your small group discussions, avoid authoritarian, dogmatic, or absolute comments and criticisms—especially when the criticism is of the person who makes a statement rather than the content of the statement. Similarly, the stronger the emotional tie the speaker has to a statement, the more likely she will hear criticism of that statement as personal. For example, if a single parent feels pride and accomplishment in the job of parenting she has been doing and then hears someone she respects say, "Single parents will raise troubled children," the statement includes a strong personal criticism as well as a prediction.

Authoritarian, dogmatic, or absolute comments leave little room for discussion:

> It snows every Christmas.
> No politician is honest.
> All charitable organizations are frauds.
> There is no reason to be poor.

Unless a person turns those statements back to the speaker with a reflective, "Hmm . . . Tell me why you think that," the conversation is then forced into a mode of refutation and argument or correction: "It didn't snow on Christmas in 1972, remember?" If the statements are made as personal observations or speculations, then discussion can continue in a productive fashion. "It seems to me that single parents have more troubled children than intact couples" is a launchpad for discussion. "I have a hard time finding a charitable organization I can feel good about" opens conversation without the need for a respondent to refute the statement or to be defensive about an organization in which he works.

Learning to Deal Openly and Honestly with Emotion

At some time, small group members will likely hear the statement, "I can't talk about that; I might cry." If a group is functioning well and has reached a reasonable level of maturity, the tears of a member will be as acceptable in the group as the laughter or the smiles of a shared joy. Reaching the point where tears are acceptable is difficult for most groups. In part, this is because, for many of us, it is not OK to cry—alone or with others.

I used to say that one group task or skill was to become comfortable with emotion. A member of the small group I am in challenged that statement and offered an alternate goal, which I have embraced: learn to deal openly and honestly with emotion—both your own and that of others. Incidentally, the challenge and the rephrased skill statement came from a man in the group—a retired U.S. Air Force officer who also happens to be the county sheriff.

At some point, the group may want to devote a session or two (or more) to discussion of questions such as, when do I cry? or what do I do when I am about to cry? Talking about crying is easier than crying in front of others. A discussion about crying may also want to cover the question, what do I do when someone else cries?

We learned lessons as children about crying (or any strong emotion). What does it show? What does it mean? What happens to us when we do cry? Those lessons will usually be found alive and well in our adulthood. Your small group will no doubt discover different triggers and meanings of tears for men and women. Responses to strong emotion will likely provide you with material for several discussions. The corollary discussions about how we respond when someone else cries (or yells or hits or walks away from trouble or the like) will be equally productive.

Crying is not the only strong emotion to be experienced in a group. Anger, fear, guilt, joy, and sadness will be present from time to time. How the group deals with strong emotions will say a lot about the nature and maturity of the group.

The guidelines for working with strong emotions in a group are as follows:

- Listen to the emotion being expressed.
- Don't change the subject to avoid the strong emotion.
- Name the emotion as you hear it.
- Don't tell a person, "You shouldn't feel that way."
- Accept the speaker's emotion without saying you feel worse, better, or the same.
- Use your own emotions to try to understand the speaker and to communicate your understanding to them without taking anything away from what he or she is saying.

Examining what you do in the presence of strong feelings is important in understanding how to respond to other people who are expressing emotions. If you know that you usually shy away from emotion, being quiet and listening to another may require extra effort. If you know that your tendency is to leap in and make other people feel better when they are in emotional pain, then it is important to figure out why you must do that and then intentionally work to let other people express their feelings without you taking over and changing their direction. These are important topics to discuss with other group members—for example, "When I see someone struggling with his emotions, I have this strong urge to jump in and make everything OK for him." Let the group members know how you react. Find out how they react—and discover what the best processes are for your group.

Maintaining Confidences

Nothing will cause a group to quit growing more quickly than a broken confidence. To hear something outside the group that someone said in a group that covenanted to maintain confidentiality will disrupt the group's functioning. Regaining the level of trust that had existed prior to the breach of confidence will take a lot of hard work and may be impossible.

Many people can describe an experience of having a confidence betrayed—whether in a small group or in other conversation. Often the person who is unwilling to share in a group carries a painful experience of a broken confidence. Experience tells the person that it's better to be quiet and not share what she would like to say than to make a statement that might be echoed outside the group a day, a week, or months later.

Holding private or personal information about another person is difficult for many people. Passing along another's secrets is tempting. Telling that information to a person outside the group can be powerfully seductive. It's a devious way to gain some personal advantage over another person.

Small group members do not converse under the same ethical guidelines that professional counselors or therapists do. Small groups have no legal requirement to keep information confidential. Only clergy, attorneys, and physicians have legal protections dealing with privileged information. The confidentiality guidelines that cover small groups are the guidelines of personal courtesy and common sense. If someone says something to you that they request not to be repeated, then don't repeat it. The group needs to discuss confidentiality in an early session and should periodically review the covenant they make about personal information: what is said in the group stays in the group.

Telling group stories, even with disguised information, is not good to do. Thinly disguised stories often mean no disguise at all. I recall a clergyperson years ago who would frequently illustrate his sermons with statements such as, "I recently counseled a young couple in my office who struggle with their mortgage and their two small children...." Immediately, people looked around the sanctuary, and some accurate guesses were made about who fit the profile. Disguising the information was no disguise at all. The clergyman, from good intentions, was probably trying to demonstrate that he was available and was working with parishioners on critical personal matters. Perhaps he was trying to demonstrate his own competence as a helper. Perhaps he just wanted to make a point. The result was destructive of the pastoral relationship and no doubt destroyed the family's confidence in him as well as warning other parishioners not to say anything they didn't want repeated from the pulpit in some form.

Small groups can develop formal or informal norms about confidentiality. If confidentiality hasn't been agreed upon before, it can also be something which a member requests or reminds the group about when a sensitive issue is discussed: "I have something I want to say, but I need to know that it will stay in the group." Make your request public in the group.

A second confidentiality issue that arises in groups is called "siphoning." Two or more group members discussing outside of the group meeting what happened in the group siphons energy and takes a process away from the group that belong in the group. Siphoning happens most frequently when a couple or friends are in the same group. Driving home, one says, "I was so upset in the group tonight." The response is, "You didn't say a thing," whereupon the first person explains what upset them, how they were feeling, and what they would like to have said. What has happened is that the work of the group gets taken outside the group. If this pattern persists, the group will never reach its potential maturity level.

Siphoning may have one small advantage for members. As in the illustration above, one person may say something to another outside the group. If this begins a discussion that improves their relationship, then the siphon may have been beneficial for the two of them, but it probably doesn't help the group move forward. The benefit to that relationship doesn't diminish the responsibility to do one's work in the group. At the least, they should return to the group at a later meeting and explain that an issue has sparked discussion between them, share the results, and talk through how the issue could have been raised and dealt with in the group originally.

Improving the Group

As a responsible member, you can help improve your group. Whether you have a permanent leader or leadership is shared, members are the ones who make the group better. The designated leader might focus attention on how the group is functioning and how it could improve, but every member has the same opportunity and responsibility to see that the group is moving forward.

Two questions to ask when assessing how your group is doing and how it could be improved are (1) how do you see yourself functioning in the group? and (2) how do the members of the group work as a group? An "improve-the-group" session can be handled in a number of ways. Here are some ideas:

- Develop your own set of questions about group performance and use them for discussion.
- Use the list of small group skills included in this chapter and talk about how well you think you measure up on each of the skills.
- Designate a member of the group to be an observer who reports observations to the group about how they are doing individually and collectively.
- Each member writes notes to other members of the group describing your observations about how the group functions

Receiving the observations of the other members of the group can be very powerful. Note that I used the word observations rather than evaluations. If the group has matured, then the members know how to describe their observations with minimal evaluative commentary attached. Observations include what you have seen happen or what you have heard said. They do not include your interpretation of assumed reasons or what you think anyone was thinking. Observations can include a series of events you have seen take place: "When you say something, Joan will usually follow with a different idea." The observations should promote good discussion.

Self-critique is also powerful. I recall a session of a group I once belonged to where each person was asked to reflect on the following questions: what do I do that helps the group along? and what do I do that impedes the group's progress? As each person in the group answered those two questions, the other members of the group would talk about the self-statements, adding support or suggesting different emphases on what had been said. There were frequent instances when the person answering each question said things that surprised the rest of the group—and, for the group as a whole, the discussion was very productive. I know that my own statement to the group about how I thought I impeded the group's progress was refuted in part (with observational data), and I learned some things about how a discussion style that I have (asking questions that I know the answer to) was not seen as helpful. The group wanted statements from me, not questions.

Group Goals

What are the goals of your group? You may have begun as a very informal discussion group, a social group, a new member group, a task group, a Bible study group. Did you begin the group with a stated goal? How about an unstated goal? Have you had an opportunity to voice those unstated goals at any time?

Formally structured groups often fly their mission statement as a flag or banner in some public place. Our church prints the mission statement on every Sunday bulletin. It is on a banner hung in the sanctuary, and it appears on church stationery as well as on the home page of our Web site. Other structured groups may recite an opening pledge that contains a goal. Small discussion groups are less likely to do that, but they most certainly have goals. The goals of an individual member may not be the same as the goals of other members. Unless made public, these goal conflicts may go unidentified—but can be problematic.

I suggest a periodic review of the group's goals. Early on the group can agree to review its goals every six months, for example. Someone in the group can take responsibility for reminding members that it's time to do a goal review. Another way goal reviews can be triggered is if a member of the group or the designated leader senses the group has drifted away from its stated goals and simply offers that observation. Groups might also review their goals after they have finished a project, a study, or at some other natural break in their work together.

Drifting away from goals is not bad in itself. The group may decide that the initial reason for coming together has changed and new goals have emerged. In the spirit of making informal norms more formal, I suggest that goals be public. It certainly helps members of the group explain to others what the group is about. The group that began with a goal of becoming better acquainted with other new people in the congregation might find that the goal has been met, and a new operational goal emerges—finding ways to deepen members' spirituality, provide mutual support, and do service. If so, then state it publicly to the group—and, if appropriate, to others.

Goals for groups in congregations often are reflected in the original name of a group. Newcomers to congregations may look at the names of different church groups and wonder if they fit in with "The 39ers" (who all appear to be 60 or more), "The Bowlers" (who never bowl), or "The Pairs" (many of whom seem to be single). I caution against attaching goal names to groups if the goal is likely to change or if the name is time limited in some way—especially if the group continues for several years.

A good exercise for members of a small group is to have each individual in the group write what they perceive as the group goal on a card. The cards can be placed in a hat and each person then draws a card, reads the goal statement, and then speaks in support of that goal statement as if they had written it themselves. The exercise will help people state and refine their own perspective of what the group is about, and it promotes clarity and mutual understanding among the members, who may have assumed they knew each person's views.

Losing and Gaining Members

Every group that continues through more than a few meetings is likely to experience changes in membership through attrition or recruitment. Depending on how the group is created—open ended or closed, fixed membership or flexible, time limited or continuing—the way that members leave and new members come in is a critical issue for the group.

When members leave a group, it is important for people to understand why they left. The reason may be clear—a job transfer, a move, an inflexible time schedule. It may be unclear; a person misses a meeting, then another, and quietly just disappears. Groups frequently will spend time speculating on why the member is absent—occasionally, more time will be spent on the absent member than when the member is present. The person's departure may be saying something about how the group has functioned, which is important for the group—individually and collectively—to know in order to make corrective steps.

Years ago I was a member of a men's group that had met weekly for several months. One member failed to show up for several meetings. The discussion in three successive meetings tended to focus on the absent member: "Where is Pete?" "What's wrong with Pete?" "Do you suppose that Pete . . .?" Finally, one member said, "I'm tired of this. We've spent most of three meetings talking about someone who's not here, talking about information we don't have, speculating about Pete's thinking instead of discussing any other topic. If we want to know where Pete is, then we should ask him or else drop the subject." The group paused and acknowledged we had been breaking one of our own rules—not talking about people not in the group. A member agreed to make an appointment with Pete to find out what was wrong and to ask Pete to come to the group and explain the issues that led to his absence.

A personal note here: I recently met with one of the members of that group and asked, "What sort of recollections do you have about the men's group we were in together?" His immediate response was to talk about the "Pete" episode—this, 17 years after the event. His recollections were the same as mine.

Finding the real reasons a member is absent may require that someone in the group have a heart-to-heart talk with the missing member. However, in the spirit of keeping the group's work in the group, the conversation will be more productive if the group will make an effort to invite the missing person to be part of a shared discussion about his or her absence. If the group has developed a sense of trust and openness, it may be possible for missing members to be honest with the group—the group didn't meet their personal, emotional, spiritual, or intellectual needs; they had other things that became more important; they were not stimulated by the discussions; they felt ignored and their ideas were discounted in discussions. The group needs to know because the person has been a part of their corporate life and to disconnect without explanation diminishes both the person and the group.

New members also need special attention. Any group that has a history together will develop its own language, knowledge base, jokes, and norms. A new member who comes to the group and hears people talking humorously about an event that they didn't participate in can quickly feel left out. This is the time when the members of the group, particularly the leader or the caretaker or the includer in the group, need to be alert and explain why "trimming trees" is a funny phrase to everyone except the new person.

When I used to train Girl Scout leaders, I would take advantage of situations where people came late to the sessions. Often, if the training was a day-long session, I could count on one or two new people arriving after lunch. I would begin the afternoon session with a focused discussion on some aspect of the morning session, and, after a few minutes of this, I would pause, go to the new people, and ask them how they felt during the previous discussion. Inevitably, they would describe feeling left out, a little stupid for not knowing what was going on, and even wishing they hadn't come to the training. My point had been made, and I encouraged group members to consider the experience of new scouts who joined an existing troop. The same integration process is important for congregations to think about when visitors come or new members join. Being mindful of new people and being inclusive, not exclusive, in language and action is an important goal of every small group.

Do You Still Want to Be a Member?

Looking at the instructions listed above, some may say, "It's too complicated. I'll just skip small group membership." I hope not. And although the list of skills may appear daunting, you already possess many of them, and they can all be acquired with practice. The benefits outweigh the effort required to attain and maintain the skills required to be a good group member.

Your life can be enriched through the connections you develop with others in a group. The exchange of information and exploration of values, issues, and beliefs with a group of fellow congregants will give you roots and connections. Those connections within one small group can enable you to reach out and connect beyond your group to others in your congregation. Like yeast, your connections expand. Envision a congregation of connected members infused with an invitational culture, and become excited with the possibilities that result.

Chapter 5

◉ Problems in Groups

This chapter is intentionally titled "problems in groups," not "problem groups." Problems do arise, but they come about because of things people do. To label a group "a problem" misidentifies what is wrong and doesn't suggest how it can be fixed. Of course, if you have some responsibility for the small group program in your church, there may be times you throw up your hands in exasperation and name a particular group as "the problem group." I hope that isn't often. If you have done that, sit back and think about the specific behaviors in the group that result in your concern. Then you will most likely be able to find a solution.

This chapter presents several kinds of difficult situations for consideration by leaders of small groups and for planners of your church's small group program: (a) concerns about ways people in the group function that can be addressed by leaders or members and (b) difficulties that seem to be natural occurrences in long-term groups. I have included a few suggestions for working with each of the problem behaviors.

Problems for Groups

Members can help groups function well or they can upset everything a group is trying to do. You can probably make

a list of the things people do in groups that result in your not
wanting to be in a group—especially when you think about a
person's particularly obnoxious behaviors. Keep in mind that
it is not an obnoxious person but a person who exhibits obnoxious behavior in the group that makes us struggle with a
group experience. As a leader or a facilitator of a small group,
you must be alert to the behaviors that reduce the group's
effectiveness.

If you are involved in planning your church's small group
program, when training potential leaders have them make lists
of the kinds of behaviors they have experienced and know or
believe will be upsetting to a group. Even more important,
ask potential leaders to identify the particular behaviors they
anticipate will be difficult for them to manage when they are
facilitating a group.

Group leaders should have enough self-awareness to (a)
know what kinds of behaviors bother them the most, (b) know
how they have dealt with those kinds of behaviors in other
group settings as members or leaders, and (c) understand how
those destructive behaviors can reduce the effectiveness of a
group. Leaders have to know how the problematic behaviors
of others affect them personally before they attempt to remedy
those behaviors in a group.

Make your own list. Some of the following behaviors would
appear on many lists:

- dominant or monopolizing talk
- nonparticipation
- changing topics prematurely
- differential responses
- conflict with the leader

In addition, you may have your own issues that can be
problematic for you in a group, such as:

- disliking a person
- changing personal priorities

- "needy" members
- negative talk

After you have developed a list of distressing behaviors, explore ways that each of the problems might be managed in a group. A few helpful strategies that address the problem behaviors are included below. You can expand the list with your own ideas.

Dominant or Monopolizing Talk

Dominant or monopolizing talk creates difficulties for most groups and their leaders. Mature groups can deal with people who dominate the conversation by utilizing some of the self-checks suggested in the previous chapter on being a group member. Less experienced groups usually rely on the leader to help manage the dominant talker.

The leader begins by observing how the members of the group react to dominant talkers. When a person dominates the conversation, do the other members begin to fidget, look bored, suddenly need to excuse themselves to get coffee, yawn, or otherwise show they are disconnecting from the group? The leader also watches the dominant talkers to identify patterns in their conversation. Do they have a habit of saying something three times in slightly different ways whenever they speak to a point? Are they usually the first person to answer a question? Do they provide much more information than is needed in explaining anything? Are they more dominant with regard to certain subjects? Do they engage certain people in the group more vigorously than others? This list could go on, but the key for the leader is to be observant—what are the dominant talkers doing? After discerning patterns in a dominant group member's behavior, the leader can more easily decide the best way to proceed.

People bring lifelong discussion habits to their group. Do not expect those deeply embedded styles to change with a simple shared observation—nor expect people will control dominant talking behavior through self-reflection. Many of us know people who may preface their comments with a warning that they are going to dominate the conversation for the next several minutes: "You know me, when I get started talking, I just can't stop. I know I shouldn't do it, but my mother called me 'Motor Mouth' and it fits, and...." Having raised the monopolizing flag high, the person will continue unabashedly, long past the point when anyone else is listening. In these cases, leaders can respond quickly and assertively to the speaker's preamble and could say, "Then let me interrupt you." A courageous leader (or a group member) might even say, "Would you like to get away from the 'motor mouth' reputation here?"

Leaders have their own style of facilitating groups. At one end is the very unobtrusive observer who lets a group go wherever it wants; at the other end of the spectrum is the controller who directs the group and informs them how and what they are doing. "Let me interrupt you" comes from a style somewhere in between. Leaders do have license to be a bit more assertive with a group, particularly if they are external leaders who are on a time-limited assignment. Consider some of the following leader responses to dominant speakers—from the less intrusive to the more controlling:

> Could someone else respond?
> Who else has a comment about that?
> I'd like to hear others speak to that issue.
> I think you've made your point.
> Do you believe you're being understood?
> You seem to have a lot to say about this. Do you want to hear others?
> Can I remind the group about the guideline that we try to give each person equal airtime?
> I've noticed that you've had about half the discussion time tonight.
> Other people are not getting a chance to talk.
> Put a cork in it! (Not really, but sometimes it feels good to consider the possibility.)

Some leaders may be inclined to take a dominant talker aside and quietly explain how control of airtime is affecting the group. My preference is that discussions of individual behavior and its effect on the group take place within the group. Doing it this way requires more skill as a leader and more maturity on the part of the group, but it is consistent with use of the group as a place to refine interpersonal skills. However it is done, the issue of a dominant talker needs to be addressed or the group life will be shortened considerably as membership declines.

Nonparticipation

Less disturbing for the group but of equal concern for the leader are silent members. Their silence is seldom disruptive, but it is more difficult to interpret—by the leader or by other members of the group. In much of contemporary culture, silence implies consent. Elements of the silent-member issue were discussed in the previous chapter about response styles. But how do leaders respond to people so silent that they seem not to be present?

In your role as leader, try not to make assumptions about why a person is silent in a group but to understand the silence. A productive discussion topic is to talk about participation levels in the group. A quiet person in the group may say, "I've always been comfortable just listening to others. I process and make my decisions without conversation, just a lot of thinking." A very different point of view might be, "I don't want to talk, because you'll all think I'm stupid." In both cases, it certainly would be important for the silent person, the leader, and the others in the group to understand the history behind those statements so that group members can know their colleagues better. That may call for another group discussion topic: how did I (we) develop our patterns of communication? The number of times someone spoke out in her family or elementary school only to be criticized or ridiculed for what she said may have had a profound effect on the way she communicates as an adult. Everyone has a reason; every behavior has a cause.

There are leader techniques for helping reluctant talkers speak. The "go-around-the-circle" device says quite loudly that everyone will get a chance to speak. Further, the procedure communicates that you will be expected to speak when it is your turn. For some people, this pressure can be unbearable as their turn approaches. Groups are well advised to develop a norm that it is acceptable to pass if a member does not want to share at that point. Have the "go-around" start at different places in the circle each time and provide some variability—do not always move clockwise, for example. The invitational technique can be gently used: "I invite you to share."

The alternative to going around the circle is to let people speak at random. This is where the dominant talker shines and the reluctant talker breathes a momentary sigh of relief: "At least I won't have to say anything, especially if Old Dominator keeps it up for as long as usual." The random or self-selected speaking order can also threaten reluctant talkers. They may feel increased pressure as the conversation builds, because when they finally must speak, all the good things to say will have been said. Or, rather than feeling pressure to speak, they might wait until last to avoid contributing: "Everything good has been said, so I won't have anything to say." Frequently, reluctant talkers add a comment when it is finally their turn such as, "I agree with what's been said."

Leaders can work with silent or reluctant members just as they can work with dominant members. Moving from a general invitation to the group (less threatening) to a direct request to the silent person (more threatening), a leader might comment:

Has everyone who wants to been able to speak to this issue?

I don't think we've heard from everyone.

We haven't heard from [name] yet.

[Name], do you want to speak to this topic?

[Name], what are your thoughts on this topic?

Members of the group can also encourage reluctant talkers with their requests to hear what they have to say. Asking for input using self-statements, such as "Doug's views are important to me (or to the group)" is more helpful than "Doug, you haven't said anything yet." A more direct and less confrontational request would be, "Doug, I'd like to hear from you—your views are important to me."

Leaders must remember that silent people have their reasons for being silent. To force a person to participate may be too uncomfortable for them in a group setting. At the same time, members may view someone who is silent as not involved—or even that their silence is judgmental (another interpretation of silence). Silence requires some thought and discussion.

Changing Topics

Nearly every group has at least one person who frequently seems to change the topic of discussion. In many instances, the person changes the topic away from something important that may be too close to them. At other times, the person may not listen to the conversation closely enough to stay on topic, so whatever comes out of his mouth is something new—almost as if the topic changer is doing a monologue rather than being part of a group discussion.

Topic changers present a moderate issue for group leaders. The simplest way to deal with them is for the leader to make an observation: "I don't think we had finished with the last topic, have we group?" The members of mature groups will handle topic changers without the leader's intervention, but if their skills aren't at a high level, the leader may need to be a bit more assertive: "That sounds like a new topic. Can we stick with the other one for a while?"

An even more assertive leader intervention is to observe, "You just introduced a new topic with that statement. Is there a reason you'd rather not talk about the previous topic?" This leader intervention puts the issue of topic changing squarely in the lap of the changer. It is confrontational and asks the changer to look at reasons for her own behavior.

Some people would advocate that the leader, or someone else, take the topic changer aside and describe what her behavior is doing to the group. My belief is that this sort of process best takes place in the group. A skillful leader can do it in a way that benefits both the topic changer and the others in the group. It need not be done in a disrespectful fashion. It could be as simple as calling attention to what the person has done by asking, "Are you aware that by changing the topic just now the flow of conversation in the group seems to have changed?"

Making assumptions about why people change topics is risky for leaders. For example, if the leader says, "Are you uncomfortable with the previous topic?" this is presumptive on the part of the leader and should be avoided unless the leader has enough observational data to support the hypothesis about discomfort. It is better for the leader not to make any assumptions about why topic changers do what they do. If the reason is important to the leader or a member of the group, then ask the person who changes the topic. It is also possible that the topic changer is not aware that she often changes the topic. The person who is unaware of her own behavior or the reasons for her behavior may require a more delicate approach in the group.

Differential Responders

In group discussions, some people respond more intently to the statements of one person than they do another. In particular, differential responding becomes an issue if the difference in response to statements reflects such things as gender or racial bias, perceived status, or personal history. When people begin to give more attention or importance to one person's statements because of class or other arbitrary designations, they have taken something away from the rest of the group and have been unfair to the person who has been ignored.

The group I am a part of recently had a discussion about the way women's statements are not valued. One woman in the group who has been on numerous governing boards and committees described how she has frequently made statements that were ignored by others only to have a male make the same or similar statement later and have it be valued. Other women in the group validated her observation with their own similar experiences.

My spouse and I have had frequent discussions about how my statements are valued by others more quickly than hers—especially when my degree, title, or position is made public. We have had some laughs about this, remembering a time when we were invited to a gathering where we knew no one present. We were both being ignored until someone who knew me entered and addressed me with the "Dr." in front of my name. Suddenly several people turned to us, wanting to engage us (me) in conversation. Needless to say, we were less interested in engaging them at that point than we might have been earlier in the evening.

Differential responding is not the same as giving weight to a person's remarks because they have legitimate expertise. I will listen to my financial advisor's opinion about retirement funds more intently than my grocer. Or if I want to know about the trees in my yard, I will ask my fishing partner—a scientist specializing in forest ecology.

Personal history can relate to differential responding, especially if the people in a group are couples or if two members have a relationship outside the group—employees, a history of committee work together, or similar experience. If the leader observes one person ignoring the statements of a partner or if one person usually criticizes statements of the same individual, it is an issue for the leader to address if the group doesn't deal with it. The response pattern may have developed over many years of being together. Small groups in churches are not marriage therapy groups; however, they are appropriate places for couples or coworkers to examine their communication patterns with others who share an interest in the topic.

Addressing differential responding is most easily handled with a leader observation: "I notice that when women in the group make statements, you frequently [describe the behavior: for example, laugh, don't respond, disagree, or the like]." It is more delicate for the leader when the issue is wrapped in personal history. "I notice that when your spouse [friend, coworker, or the like] makes a statement, you often close your eyes and make a face. What does that mean?" Be prepared, as a leader, for an intense discussion that other couples or friends in the group will join when this kind of observation is made.

This discussion may provoke some generalizations such as, "Men never..." or "Women always..." It may be an opportunity for the group to challenge such generalizations. The discussion in chapter 4 about dogmatic or authoritarian statements may be helpful if such claims are made.

Leader Conflict

Individuals in a group, or the entire group, can have conflict with a leader's style. And leaders can have conflict with group members. Conflict with a leader is most likely to occur when a leader is attempting to move the group in a direction members are reluctant to explore. This may happen when an external leader has been sent or invited to a group to help them work on issues that have been blocking the group's progress. For internal leaders, conflict between the leader and group members is most likely to occur when the leader carries some history of unresolved conflict with one or more members.

Most of us will do more to avoid conflict than to manage it. In small groups, conflict reflects power struggles of some kind—either between or among members or between the leader and a member or members. Some people who regularly work with conflict use the word manage instead of resolve when discussing conflict, because they believe that true conflict is not resolved, only managed to the point that it doesn't interfere with progress. Left unmanaged, conflict will destroy group processes and goals.

How a leader works with conflict or resistance depends on how and why the leader is in the group—whether the leader is external or internal, short- or long-term, invited by the group or sent. At the beginning of their time together, the leader and the group should reach clarity on the reason the leader is present and on the functions to be performed: "I'm here for four sessions at your request to help you work with some communication issues you have identified. My role will be to observe and comment, not to criticize or instruct." Group members might welcome a leader who comes to help the group through a specific process issue. Or they might resist a time-limited leader, which means the leader must focus on leadership before moving on to other group dynamics.

A leader who is invited to a group, even when the task is to help the group work on conflict among members, usually has an easier task than if sent to a group. However, even in the case of an invited leader, the leader and the group need to be clear about the reason the invitee is there and how the leader is expected to function during the time with the group.

Most difficult for leaders in small groups are situations where the leader has a history of conflict with one or more members—not an uncommon situation in many churches. It is particularly problematic if the leader senses personal feelings of hostility, anxiety, frustration, or anger rising during group sessions. In those situations, leaders need to have a place to process the feelings they experience—a small group for leaders of groups will help a church program succeed. It is important for leaders to talk through the issues they have experienced with members of a group they are facilitating. If the conflict is intense between group members, then the church needs to consider how members are chosen for or assigned to various groups.

Leaders need to be open with group members about the way they deal with conflict and to model what they hope the group can eventually do for itself: "I sense some hostility in the group. Can we talk about that?" "I notice a lot of silence after I make a suggestion. Are you having problems with my leadership?" Or, "It seems you're not as open and free with your conversation tonight. Is there some conflict which we need to talk about?" Chapter 7 includes a more extensive discussion of conflict.

Problems for Members

Individual members of groups could make a long list of signs indicating they have problems in or with the group. If you as a member of a group put words to your feelings about attending the group, what appears? "I feel bored," "I've lost interest," "I'm uncomfortable with [name]," "I feel ignored," "I think we talk only about petty issues," "I have too much other stuff to do." Each of these responses, or others you might make, is not a problem as much as it is a symptom of issues that need to be addressed. As a group member, you must consider to what extent the issue is your own and to what extent the issue is one for the group to attend to.

Disliking a Person

Among the examples in the list above, "I'm uncomfortable with [name]" is perhaps the most critical. Once you have met with 10 or 11 other people for several sessions, it is not likely you will care for each person in absolutely the same way. Preferences and dislikes will emerge. The extent to which your preferences for one person and your dislike for another begin to interfere with the way you participate as a member, or, worse, the way the group is able to function, determines how essential it is to find a way to deal with your likes and dislikes. The starting point for working with different likes and dislikes is careful examination of your own behaviors to determine what it is that draws you to one person and pushes you away from another.

Your theology may suggest that you love everyone equally, but that does not mean the way a person behaves or how or what they say about issues does not bother you. You may have learned to suffer in silence and believe you must not say anything about your dislikes. Mother may have said, "If you can't say anything nice, don't say anything at all." Over time, this childhood message may have become a mode of operation and you are not able to express criticisms of any kind. But if your dislike gets in the way of your being a good group member, it is incumbent on you to find a way to work with the issue. Choosing to be absent or to leave the group is not a good solution. I don't suggest that you walk into group at some meeting and announce, "I don't like you." I do suggest that you tell the group you are struggling with your feelings and that causes you to lose enthusiasm.

We can dislike people for a variety of reasons. Something in their behavior may be distressing; their values and beliefs may be contrary to your own and you haven't found a way to coexist without tension; or something about the person disturbs you, but you just can't describe what it is. It may be that they remind you of someone—"You look and act just like my ex, and we never got along." They may have personal habits or mannerisms that carry unpleasant memories for you—"I am not a hugger, and I really feel invaded when anyone grabs me to try to be affectionate."

The two short illustrations above are examples of how behaviors or characteristics can be described in a way that lets a person know there is tension between you. It is much more difficult if you feel strong dislike but cannot describe the source. If this is the case, addressing the tension may require that you sit with someone and talk about your dislike in order to clarify your description. For the sake of your comfort level in the group and for the effectiveness of the group, you need to put the behaviors of the person you dislike into specific terms.

When you can say to yourself, "I don't care as much for [name] because of what she does or because of who she looks like or because of her beliefs and values," then you are getting closer to being able to find a way to make your experience in the group more tolerable. In the end, if the intensity of your dislike and the inability to describe reasons is so strong, you may need to leave the group. On the other hand, if you can give voice to the specifics of your dislike, you may find you are not alone.

Changing Priorities

Individual or personal priorities evolve over time. Having joined a small group that has developed a set of goals and a customary method of operating, you may find that the things that were once important to you have changed over time. Or you may find that certain religious, political, social, family, health, or personal issues grow in importance for you in a way that is not in synch with the rest of the group.

The critical question for you when your priorities change is, how are you going to reconcile those differences with the members of the group? The answer is to take the issue to the group, discuss the change openly, and make your decisions about what to do. Whether you make your decision publicly in the group or privately after exchanging views in a regular gathering with the other members, the group needs to be aware of the reasons for your decision. To disappear quietly, without explanation, is not helpful for the group and is a bit unfair on your part.

Needy Members

Life is probably best characterized as a continuous series of changes resulting in highs and lows that come with little warning. During the highs, it's nice to have a place to share your exuberance with people who know and understand you. And during the lows, it's even better to have that group of friends who can listen and understand. A small group can provide that support.

A point may come when one person's needs are so intense or so persistent that the group finds it has no other life. In that situation, a difficult decision must be made about whether or not the group continues to give itself to the one person. A person with needs and issues more critical or chronic than the group is prepared to deal with creates a real dilemma—the group may want to give support, but the needs are beyond the scope of a friend network. Small groups in churches are not therapy groups. The group may then become involved in helping the individual find the appropriate support for his issues outside the group.

Suggesting that a person seek professional help with personal issues is not a sign of rejection or a lack of care. In fact, it may be a strong expression of love and support to say to another, "I am concerned about you and would like to help, but I believe you need more than I can provide. I really want you to see a professional counselor about the things we've been discussing."

Negative Talk

Most people have had the experience of being in a group when an idea is presented only to have it die immediately when someone says, "That won't work" or "You're wasting your time" or "We tried that twice, and it didn't work." When the negative comment comes from someone who is respected, who has a long history with your church, or who is perceived as a powerful person, it can cause conversation to stop quickly. When the overall conversation in a group tends to be negative or cynical, one can be assured that the group members will quickly lose interest, fade away, or become combative as soon as possible.

Negative talkers are difficult to deal with in groups, especially when they seem so potent or their negativity seems well founded. If a person with expertise in a topic is negative, it is even more difficult for the uninformed person to continue the conversation. Countering them with your own positive comments may only escalate the negativity. Continuing to be optimistic about an idea or continuing any discussion is hard when every response is a litany of negative remarks.

For small groups, the important thing to do is to help the negative talker become aware of how their style of reacting affects other people. Therefore, the strategy is for members or leaders to stick to first-person statements and describe what the negative comments have done to them. If in a discussion you hear another "That won't work," helpful responses can be:

> I don't feel that negatively about the idea.
>
> I get a little defensive when my ideas are shot down so quickly.
>
> After you make such a strong negative comment, I don't feel like suggesting anything else.
>
> I hear your comments as very negative. Could you possibly see some of the positive in [the topic under discussion]?
>
> Ouch—I feel like my idea just got shot down with a big gun.

Groups can develop signals as quick shorthand or a sign to let others in the group know what is happening to a listener. The group I am in has adopted the word "ouch" as a quick signal to others that a statement has hit a sensitive spot. In most instances, the speaker has not intended to hurt another person, so the "ouch" lets the group be aware that what was said hit a tender spot with a listener. The effect of saying "ouch" out loud is to raise the level of awareness among people in the group, particularly the speaker, that people respond differently to various words and that some people in the group may have a lot of strong feelings attached to words or ideas.

The Problem-Free Group

This chapter may give the impression that so many problems exist in small groups that getting started in one is a bad decision. On the contrary, small groups present wonderful possibilities to work through a variety of life issues among a group of supportive friends. Rather than ignore the glitches and stumbling blocks that frequently are present in small groups, this chapter has openly acknowledged they do exist—just as the suggestion is made throughout the text that it is better for individuals to name and work through problems rather than to hide them or pretend they don't exist. If the small group in which you are a member has no problems at all with any of the items mentioned above (or others), please call me. Perhaps the age of miracles hasn't passed.

Chapter 6

◉ What to Do About...?

Once small groups are up and running, the question for members is, what are we going to do? Or, as situations arise, what are we going to do about [situation a, b, c, . . . z]? The answer: whatever you decide. This chapter provides some suggestions about situations, activities, issues, and matters that are common to many groups, with illustrations from the small group I am in.

What's to Eat?

Can it be a church meeting if there is no food? Food is an important part of the sessions for the small group I am in. For 16 years we have been meeting in member homes, rotating the location so that no one has the group two weeks in a row. Our meetings begin with a gathering, coffee, and some "munchie," usually a dessert, so the members know to skip dessert with their Wednesday evening meal.

Food does provide a social lubricant. Our food selections range from the simple to the elaborate, from store-bought to homegrown. Over food, our greetings and catching-ups begin.

A good idea? Probably so, except in those situations where food preparation becomes competitive, an inconvenience, or a financial hardship. As a group, we have grown to accept a wide range of offerings, and the standards change over time. As a retired person, I usually have time to prepare something when the group is at our home. One evening, when we were pressed for time, I provided ice cream bars, whereupon one person said, "I'm so glad you did that. I've wanted to do it for some time." We hadn't realized until then that the food standard had become so rigid.

Has Everyone Checked In?

Groups need to develop some form of regular check-in. Check-in usually amounts to talking about events or activities that have taken place since the group last met. Check-in can become long and laborious if every person must tell every detail of every activity (see chapter 4 for "TMI" discussions), but groups can deal with this potential problem in a variety of ways—limiting the time or asking people to share just one most-important item with the group, for example.

Check-in time can come at the beginning or at the end of a group session or it can last the entire session. In our small group, following our 15-minute gathering time for coffee and dessert, the leader will often say up front what we are going to do about check-in. "Let's spend 45 minutes in discussion tonight and hold our check-in time until the end of our time together." Or "We haven't all been together for several weeks and there have been some vacations and trips, so let's check in first and use the time remaining tonight for our lesson." If a person comes to a meeting with a particularly heavy issue for which he or she needs additional time, then it could be a standard procedure for people to request that time at the start of the session.

Check-in can be focused on our response to an event the group has been a part of in the preceding week. Our group has gone through weddings of children, illnesses of children, family crises, personal health issues, job changes, and all manner of things that can happen to 12 people over the course of 16 years. Check-in might be initiated with a request that each person share some thought about an event we have attended.

Another form of focused check-in is to name an issue or condition that is the central point of the check-in. For example, "For check-in tonight, talk briefly about your progress toward a personal goal." Focused check-ins can be as wide ranging as the leader is creative. They can also be time limited: "You have 58 seconds each for check-in." Hold the stopwatch and see what happens when people must either squeeze their thoughts in to the allotted time or work to fill the 58 seconds. This kind of check-in usually triggers a request for people to tell the rest of the story later in the session if the stopwatch cut them off before they finished.

The problem with check-ins is that they expand to fill whatever time is available. That tells you people do have a need to connect. Doing that is hard unless we are willing to share what is going on with us—to have others hear our stories and to hear theirs. Consistently using all the group time for check-in is not the best use of the group's time, however, if the group has other goals—such as study, work, or discussion of issues. Striking a balance between personal sharing and sticking to "business" is also critical for task and decision groups. I have been a member of governing groups in churches where meetings were prolonged and some of the work didn't get done because the leader encouraged more check-in and personal sharing than there was time for. Small support groups are better designed for personal sharing activities but need to keep the balance of time in mind for the purposes of the group.

Who Is Going to Pray?

If a small group is a church group, shouldn't prayer be a part of the gatherings? The answer may seem obvious, but thought should be given to how the group will pray. Praying in public is enough of a problem for some people that if the expectation is that group members are at times expected to lead prayer, some people might choose not to join the group. Prayer should be an early topic of discussion for the group. Conversation might focus on questions such as, What is your experience with prayer? How do you feel when you are asked to lead a prayer? Are there times when you feel uncomfortable with prayer, either your own or that of others? When do you feel best (worst) about prayer? People in a small group can pray in a variety of ways—silent prayers, one-word prayers, listening to music, reading hymn lyrics, or using published devotional material. Your small group could study materials designed to help people learn to pray. Prayer resources are available in churches and from religious publishers.

The group I am in has developed a closing prayer routine. All those present stand in a circle, arms around each other (at least for those who aren't suffering from arthritis, ski injuries, or other health problems that prevent lifting their arms that high). The leader of the evening asks if there are special prayer requests or people or events we need to bring to attention, and then a closing prayer is offered by the leader of the evening. Sometimes the leader instead turns to someone else in the group: "Joan, would you lead us?" The person doing the closing prayer usually acknowledges some thought or idea that has been discussed during the evening. Our prayers celebrate joys and address concerns; we speak to health issues—our own and those of others. When the "Amen" echoes at the end, arms drop and someone usually says, "We can meet at our house next week." Of course, there are numerous comments then about who will be out of town, traveling, in a meeting that will cause them to be late, and the like. A few more follow-up comments to the evening's check-in may take place; then people make their way to their cars.

Prayers in a small group don't have to be limited to closing. There may be times at the beginning or middle of a session when prayer is called for. At times our group has also identified prayer partners, and individually we have made special efforts to keep that person in our thoughts through the week. Above all, the prayer routine in your group should not be something that prohibits a person from being a member.

Can We Decide on That?

Every small group makes decisions, even though the group may not be a decision-making group such as a governing board, a task group, or a planning group. The way groups make decisions is a critical element to study. Chapter 7 on conflict and decision making provides some background on individual and group decision making and suggests some discussion exercises that can be used to help a small group understand its decision-making style. There is no perfect decision-making style for a small group; however, individuals in groups and groups themselves need to understand how they make decisions in order for the group to work well together. As you are discussing decision making, you might consider: What decisions are hard and which are easy for you to make as individuals and as a group? What happens if you don't think you are included in the decision making process? Does one person tend to make decisions for the group? Your discussion could also focus on whether your decision making in the group is similar or different from decision making in your family or at work. Feeling included in decisions is an important aspect of group unity.

Are You a Hugger?

Our small group includes people who hug at the drop of a hat, while others feel awkward hugging. It is a mistake to force hugging. Watch what happens in a church service if there is a scheduled time for people to "meet and greet" or to "give hugs" to those around them. Inevitably, if everyone in the congregation is expected to hug, some people will quietly drift away, so they don't have to be invaded by the unwanted hug. Unfortunately, many congregations have not done a very good job of educating worshipers about the meaning of "sharing God's peace," which is a liturgical action proclaiming our reconciliation with one another, not a social activity. Nor have they paid attention to the personal boundary issues if people are expected to hug everyone.

Hugging is another topic for early conversation in your group. Let people know what you are comfortable with. Let them know what is uncomfortable. Nonhuggers will have their own reasons for not wanting to hug. Frequently those reasons reside in specific memories they may not have discussed with others and may not wish to discuss. Whether you explain your reasons or not is up to you, but hugging should be optional.

Where to Meet?

Our group, which includes six couples, meets in the homes of the members. We have joked over the years that our rotation means each house gets cleaned once every six weeks. And we have also talked about the ultimate sign of trust and acceptance: hosting the group and not even picking up the daily papers from the floor. We haven't reached that level yet. A woman in a small group in a church I worked with described the day she went to her group at church in dirty gardening clothes. That was the day she realized the acceptance level in her group and her comfort level had reached a new high.

The meeting place can serve to facilitate the group's discussion if the environment is one where people feel comfortable and group discussion is convenient. On the other hand, the meeting place can prohibit people from being members if the expectation is that members will take turns hosting in their home. If someone's home or apartment is not big enough for your group to meet in or if a person is embarrassed with his living space, then he might not join a group. Other reasons people might not want to host in their home might include having a spouse who is not a member of the group or having young children who might not understand that parents need private time. Older children might not have other places to go while the group meets.

Planning groups need to have a variety of meeting places in mind as they are developing initial group sessions. Sixteen years ago our group began by meeting in a classroom at church for the initial six sessions. At the end of our six sessions, we decided that meeting in homes would be more conducive to conversation, and we have done that ever since. It works for us but may not work for all.

How Often Shall We Meet?

The answer to the question, "How often shall we meet?" is "Often enough to maintain continuity, contact, vitality, and a sense of group purpose." Answers to the corollary questions, "How often is too frequent and how often is too seldom?" are "Not so often that you have no other life" and "Not so seldom that you have to wear name tags each time you meet."

When I tell people that the group I am in has met two hours a week for 16 years, the typical response is disbelief that a continuing group would have that kind of schedule. I don't suggest that small groups should meet weekly to be successful; however, I am concerned about small groups that meet monthly or even less frequently. As a group, we find that meeting weekly lets us be informed of the ongoing events in each other's life and allows time for study, reflection, discussion, and all the other things we do for a session. I believe it is important for support groups to have a balance of study and service activities, just as it is important for task and decision groups to attend to the interpersonal support so important to all the members.

As I have suggested in relation to other issues, frequency of meeting should be a serious topic for discussion. People will agree to meet as often as the meetings provide the sustenance that a small group is capable of providing. If meeting time is seen as a burden, then the schedule (or the group) is not working well and needs to be discussed by members of the group. What the members expect to receive (and give) to the group needs to be in balance with the time scheduled. If it isn't, adjustments need to be discussed.

Homogeneous or Heterogeneous Groups?

Homogeneity often makes for a smoother group start-up. For example, a group of young married couples may get started faster than an intergenerational group of married and single people. Whether your groups are homogeneous or heterogeneous in makeup may depend, in part, on the nature of your church and what you are trying to accomplish with a small group program. Much can be learned across generations and across various groupings—marital status, age, ethnicity, language, education, employment, or the like. Heterogeneous groups are certainly worth a try to increase the probability that persons who might not know each other well would have an opportunity to make connections and learn about each other.

In churches where there is a mix of both new and long-time members or where people of a race or ethnicity different from the majority of the congregation's members have joined the congregation, small group ministry is an effective means of building congregational connection. Young people may assume that being in a group of much older members will not suit them; however, as people discover through dialogue that they share common life struggles, both older and younger members may be pleasantly surprised by the beneficial results. A 12-session small group program will give people a chance to tell their stories and form connections. They may decide to continue beyond 12 sessions.

In the contemporary world of highly mobile populations, it is highly unlikely that members of any small group have experienced similar faith journeys. Even if the members have grown up in the same community and have been in the same church since childhood, individual and family differences in combination with education and experience will likely result in different theological understandings. That might be an advantage to a small group, not a hindrance. It is another place where heterogeneity can be a positive aspect of the small group's make-up.

A small group provides a wonderful place for people to tell their story. If the group is functioning well, then it is a rich experience to hear people describe differing theological perspectives, different beliefs, ways those beliefs have been acquired, times their beliefs have been questioned, and how the beliefs work in their day-to-day lives.

A few churches organize small group programs to stress compliance in doctrinal matters. I do not support use of a small group to enforce doctrinal beliefs. I do think a small group could be the place where people can study doctrine, talk about what they have been learning, and have a chance to chew over and discover personal implications of theological and doctrinal matters. I urge vigorous discussion of faith journeys, so that people can share their personal experience with others and, in the process, discover and clarify their own perspectives. In those discussions, utilize the listening skills described earlier in this book. Two people can explain their different understandings of religious belief without having to agree to a single point of view.

If planners anticipate that members of a small group might feel very uncertain about discussing theology or doctrine, then they can organize initial small groups so that they include people who are at a similar stage of faith development. On the other hand, creating diverse groups also may be very good if, for example, the group includes a wiser mentor—not someone who will dominate thinking, but one who can assist people over the hurdles and stumbling blocks inherent in "church" discussions. The goal is to develop understanding and to understand "the other."

Can We Mix Politics and Religion?

All of us have heard the expression that "politics and religion don't mix." That is not to say people in a small group could not have good discussions about politics, elections, political candidates, and governmental issues. The small group that I am in usually has one session close to election time when the voter guide is used as a discussion topic. The members of the group share information they have about candidates, ask questions of each other, and seek ways to clarify their points of concern. In similar fashion, we discuss the ballot issues being presented. No one is urged to take a particular position. In the spirit of our group, we share information and seek clarification. Your group may find other ways to explore these topics.

Does Money Make a Difference?

It would be rare for the members of any small group to be in exactly the same financial condition. Money is another of those things that can divide us. Small groups should be mindful of costs when they plan activities. One member might have child-care costs that others don't have, or some members might easily afford expensive activities that would stretch others' budgets. It may be difficult for a member to "toss in a twenty" if the group decides to take up a collection for something. Mature groups will have developed enough trust and shared information that they will know if an event is too costly for some members and will keep those issues in the forefront when planning.

Can I Bring the Children?

Children should be seen and heard; however, adults need time for themselves where they can have serious discussion with other adults who love and care for them. If churches don't provide child care for small groups, then the group should consider ways to assist those members who have children so they can be active participants. At times a small group may want to include children in discussions and activities; however, involve the whole group in planning such events.

Would You E-mail the Meeting Schedule to Me?

Most people have access to the Internet these days, but groups should not assume that everyone in a small group is wired. If everyone in a group does have e-mail, however, it can be used effectively to schedule meetings, remind people of events, and pass along information between meetings, such as illnesses, schedule changes, and reminders of things to bring or do before a next meeting.

Electronic mail is not a good place to have arguments, nor is it a medium for resolving conflict or finishing heated discussions. Neither should e-mail be used for private conversations between group members about a third member or someone who was absent.

The group I am in will frequently post a question for discussion by e-mail two days prior to our scheduled sessions. The message also serves as a reminder about where we are meeting. In writing this book, group members have used e-mail to pass along ideas for me to consider and I have sent them drafts of chapter materials.

What Shall We Talk About?

I believe that most groups of adults can decide what they would like to dig in to—ranging from exploration of personal values, beliefs about child rearing, theological ideas, the condition of the church, life transitions, or the like. If the group is not eager to develop its own discussion or lesson materials, numerous resources are available. Appendix A includes lists of discussion topics for beginning groups, more experienced groups, and mature groups. In this instance, a mature group is defined as one that has worked through some of the more critical communication issues and is able to handle conflict, strong emotional expression, differing opinions, and personal crises without becoming stressed or dysfunctional as a group.

If the group is in search of materials to use for discussion or lessons, consult the various sources listed in print and nonprint catalogs. An easy way to find materials specifically prepared for small groups is to do a Web search. If you browse for "small group ministry," you will probably have more than twenty thousand hits. "Small group ministry" plus "discussion" will produce almost two thousand hits. There are numerous Web sites with suggestions and study materials. Most religious publishing houses that carry discussion or study materials will catalog some materials under the heading "small groups."

How Do Groups End?

Contemporary culture puts much more emphasis on beginnings than it does on endings. Churches have rituals for taking in new members but may lack similar rituals for departures. Planning groups will probably spend a lot of time deciding how small groups will get started. Additional time should also be given to discussing how groups end.

Groups that agree to meet for a predetermined number of sessions have solved part of the ending problem when they begin. Groups organized to study a specific topic or carry out a project have natural ending points. When the study has been completed or the project is finished, the group has a logical ending point. Endings should include some closing ritual. Whether it is a formal participation in communion or just a session or two set aside to review and reflect on the life of the group, a closure activity is important. Plan to talk about what the group has done, what relationships have been built, what people have learned about themselves and others, and what the group has meant in their lives. A group might create an object, symbol, photo, or token as a symbolic remembrance of its life together.

It is not uncommon, however, for small groups to reach the initial ending point and look for ways to continue. When they do continue, provide ways to acknowledge that an initial goal has been reached and also to say farewell to members who choose not to continue with the group. One church started a small group program with each group initially meeting for 12 sessions. As part of the final session, the minister attended and celebrated communion with the group. Some of the groups then continued beyond the 12 sessions, but they each had a sense of closure, and members were free to continue or depart.

Open-ended groups have a more difficult time deciding when to end. Quiet attrition, with members drifting away without explanation, is not a satisfactory way to end. That would be as if a group of employees failed to show up for work and no one was curious about what contributed to their leaving. Unfortunately, quiet attrition may be a common way for small groups to end. Groups that try to hang on to an original goal long past the time that it is viable will struggle to retain members; they either need to revise their goals or end—even though ending may be difficult to do.

Whether a group agreed to meet for a specific number of sessions or began as an open-ended group, plan appropriate farewell ceremonies when individual members depart. It is a time for members to acknowledge what the person's presence has meant to them—individually and collectively. And it is a time when the departing member can do the same for the rest of the group.

Some groups may end using the "yeast" model. That is, they bring their group to a close with the intention that the individual members will go out and create other groups. Some small group programs in churches always have a group leader and a leader-in-training, so that when the group ends a new leader will be ready to start a new group. In the model suggested throughout this book, every member could be considered a leader in training, and the multiplication effect will increase several-fold.

A concluding activity for a small group could be to create its own ending ritual. The ritual could celebrate the life and accomplishments of the group as well as bless the future of the participants as they leave the group. They might be going on to create additional groups or they might be in situations where they are not likely to see each other again. Plan closing rituals to help members with the transitions to whatever follows in their lives.

What Else?

I haven't included everything that any group should consider. I have included a few issues common to most groups. Throughout this chapter, I have suggested that as issues about the group's functioning are identified they become discussion topics for the group to work out. Remember, the best solutions to issues and problems are the ones developed by the group itself.

Chapter 7

◉ Conflict and Decision Making

Two topics often overlooked in the life of small groups are conflict and decision making. Both processes involve bringing together different ideas and examining them. Conflict and decision making are also similar because many groups don't handle either of them very well. Whether the group is a small support group designed to nurture and support members or an official governing body of a church, groups benefit by giving some attention to how they handle both conflict and decision making.

There's No Conflict in Our Group!

Small groups will experience conflict (oops, there is another of those absolute statements that chapter 4 says to avoid!). It has been said that the total absence of conflict is death; however, I don't go that far. A small group can function for a fairly long time and, to the casual observer, may not seem to experience conflict, because most people learn more ways to hide or avoid conflict than they learn ways to openly work with conflict. If the group is really dealing with substantive life issues, serious discussions about concepts and values, or heavy matters of other kinds, then, in the process, members will have experienced degrees of conflict.

A productive discussion for your small group would be to examine the issue of conflict. In preparing material for this book, I prevailed on the members of the small group I am in to help me look at conflict. An early awareness in our discussion was that in the 16 years our group has been together, conflict had never been one of our Wednesday night topics. I posed several questions and topics for discussion—and, true to the 16-year history of the group, responses poured out. I present the series of questions here for your group to discuss. I don't think you have to wait 16 years before you open the dialogue.

You might begin by developing your own definition of conflict. A dictionary definition will include words such as fight, struggle, disagreement, dispute, or quarrel. A good question to ask is: what do you think of (and what do you feel) when you hear the word conflict? Answers might include: conflict of church and state, the Korean conflict, personal conflict, conflict of interest, or values conflict. Feelings might include: anxious, fearful, or flight. Examples of conflict might include: conflicts with children or parents, conflict on the job, or (I realize this one is hard to imagine) a conflict at church.

Conflict isn't just a difference of opinion. Conflict will most likely have some interpersonal dimension related to it. That is why conflict is hard to deal with; it moves away from what we think or some piece of information and gets closer to who we are. The closer the disagreement is to our basic values and beliefs, the more intense will be the feelings connected with the conflict.

I believe our small group's discussion about conflict would be similar to those of many groups. Conflicts in large organizations have been discussed extensively in the popular literature and in books on organizational development. Church conflicts can look like those of large organizations or they can look like the conflict found in most families or small groups. The questions and our group's discussion included the following:

When You Experience Conflict, What Feelings Do You Have?

This is a hard question to answer if a person has difficulty putting feelings into words. It is also a hard question to answer if a person avoids conflict so successfully that she cannot point to a conflict experience.

"Anxiety" is a frequent answer to the question about feelings associated with conflict. When people experience conflict or they anticipate they are going to experience conflict, they become anxious. Each of us will have different reactions when we feel anxious—ranging from sweaty palms and shortness of breath to a pumped-up adrenalin rush similar to what an athlete feels before a game. For many people, the anxiety that accompanies conflict is so uncomfortable that they begin to do things that ensure it won't happen again—thus the pattern of avoidance that many describe when they anticipate a conflict situation.

If your group talks about the question posed above, try to keep the conversation focused on the feelings connected with conflict. We often use the word feel when we mean think. Try to emphasize the feelings associated with conflict and make a list of the words used to describe those feelings. Keep in mind that the way each person feels when in or anticipating a conflict situation is a legitimate feeling. Our feelings are our own.

What Are Your Reactions and Responses to Conflict?

Once your group has generated its list of feelings, encourage people to look at how their feelings and behaviors are connected. Feelings don't cause behaviors, but they are associated with behavior; that is, feelings and behaviors often exist together. You do make decisions about what to do based on the feelings you have. Next have each member choose a feeling from the list the group has made and connect it to a behavior, as in the following statement: "When I feel _____ related to conflict, then I [behavior or reaction]." You will probably get a lot of responses such as:

> When I feel anxious in a conflict situation, I change the subject.
> When I feel nervous in a conflict situation, I get quiet and try to escape some way.
> When I feel threatened in a conflict, I decide to get away.

One person in our group said, "When I feel conflicted, I go analytical and wonder, 'What is going on in this situation?'"

Your discussion will probably begin with conflict situations outside the group, such as work scenarios. To talk about conflict present within the group is more threatening. At some point, you can identify this phenomenon as another example of how we usually avoid conflict: even when we talk about it, we want it to be far enough away to be safe. In this instance, I recommend that you begin by examining group conflict issues in settings other than your small group; it will permit the group to examine conflict issues and learn how they behave in those situations without having to talk about a conflict in the group. Group members can talk objectively about conflict with others rather than with the people sitting around them. The general concepts or principles of conflict can be defined and discussed. Later, you can move these same concepts and principles into the small group with more safety than if you were to focus all the conflict discussion on the group to begin with.

How Are Your Feelings or Behaviors Situation- or Person-Dependent?

People will also discuss this question more easily if they talk about conflict situations outside the group. They can identify how conflict feelings differ if the person with whom they are in conflict is a supervisor or subordinate in a work situation.

Trying to determine logical causes and effects of their different feelings and behaviors in conflict situations outside the group will be helpful.

Within a small group, if you realize that you experience the uncomfortable internal conflict feelings more frequently when one person rather than another speaks, then your feelings are signaling that the interpersonal conflict has more to do with the person than the topic. When that happens, examine your relationships to discover what in your history makes a comment from one person become a flash point when the same comment from another is received in a neutral manner.

The risk/reward ratio might be used in discussion to illustrate different conflict situations where the risk is high and the reward low—or when the reverse is true. To have a major conflict with the person who determines if you are employed or not has more risk than if the same conflict involved a peer or a stranger who had no control over your work or career. On the other hand, a conflict with a supervisor might have a high reward potential if, as a result of the conflict, a new idea or a solution to a problem were to result. Some businesses encourage a culture of conflict and challenge as a means of producing the best or the newest ideas. I don't believe a challenge climate is conducive to small support groups.

What Do You Feel When You Observe Conflict Firsthand?

This question lets people identify whether they react differently depending on how close to the center of the conflict they find themselves. Young children often describe powerful emotions when they observe their parents in conflict. Adults may squirm when they see children in conflict—whether the children are their own or not.

One member of our group talked about wanting to get away when he observed others in conflict—"I want to run," he said. Having strong feelings about conflicts you observe, even when the subject of the conflict or the outcome doesn't

affect you, comes from your ability to empathize with others—
an admirable human characteristic. Observing others in conflict might also raise for you the question of whether you
should intervene. This is another topic for small group discussion, particularly as you describe scenes from the public
arena—restaurants, shopping malls, grocery stores, or the like.
Nearly everyone can describe having watched a parent-child
interaction in public where the conflict may have bordered
on abuse. What feelings did you experience and what action
did you consider in such situations?

What Conflict Models Did You Observe or Experience as a Child?

This question is common to any discussion of adult behavior:
what we perceive, know, experience, and do often has roots
in our own childhood. This question could easily come much
earlier in your group's conflict discussion. When I posed this
question to the members of our Wednesday night group, the
answers were predictable. One person described two methods
of dealing with conflict, one observed in his father and one
in his mother. From that experience, he had resolved not to
handle conflict in the same way that his mother had during
his youth.

Another person in the group talked about having observed
a fairly regular family conflict that would start at the dinner
table when a sibling was predictably late. The childhood discomfort at watching this nightly routine resulted in her firm
resolve to not have dinner-table conflict when she became a
parent.

If most members of your small group are parents, the discussion of conflict models could continue by discussing the
conflict models you present or presented to your own children
during their youth. This question may be more personally
revealing and therefore more threatening than the ones suggested thus far. It requires self-description, self-awareness, and
discussion about personal behaviors. If your group is made up
of couples with children, the question itself raises the potential

for conflict. If one parent describes how she or he manages conflict in their family, the partner may respond, "No you don't!" This kind of statement illustrates a conflict—a difference of opinion—that can become discussion material.

Your small group may wish to extend the discussion of conflict management by examining models members see in their day-to-day world. I confess that I am greatly disturbed by the plethora of television talk shows that present people responding to conflict—often family or marital conflict—by yelling and even physical violence. The format of the shows often has someone surprising a person with a public announcement of an indiscretion or outrageous act. The reaction is intense. I am also distressed by the fact that this kind of TV show passes for entertainment, suggesting that we enjoy seeing such confrontations. Viewers—both children and adults—who may see these shows as ways to resolve unsatisfactory relationships or disagreements are acquiring an unhealthy set of behaviors.

When Has Your Small Group Experienced Conflict?

If you have had enough time to discuss conflicts outside your group, how you understand conflict, how you observed people dealing with conflict as a child, and what you tend to do when you are in conflict, then you may be ready to identify conflicts you have had in the small group. When I raised this question with the small group I am in, several people smiled and described times when they had experienced some degree of conflict only to use one of their avoidance methods—changing the subject, remaining silent, or deciding it wasn't worth it. Remaining silent may be an acceptable response if it doesn't add to the group's dysfunction over time. Personal integrity in voicing a point of view is a matter of individual choice. One behavior that more than one person described was discussing the conflict after the group session was over. This brought up a discussion of siphoning (see chapter 4).

Many church members, who have taken some of the scriptural passages about loving neighbors or living in harmony and charity with others as their absolute bywords, may still have difficulty identifying conflict situations. People in the group I am in have learned over the years what the others' beliefs and passions are. They know what topics are likely to offend or where disagreements may lurk. As a result, the group has become, to some extent, a collection of people who carefully avoid stepping on the toes of others. One result of this informal norm is that some topics never get discussed. Another is that members may choose to guard their statements about certain topics. The holding back may let the group continue to have safe dialogue, but substantive issues may be shortchanged in the process.

What Would You Change about Your Response to Conflict?

This question opens the door for people to describe their own behaviors and goals. It also permits members of the group to talk about how they can individually or collectively support a person's desired behavior change. When I raised the question in our small group, several members stated specific goals rather quickly. One person talked about his desire not to become so angry in a conflict situation, knowing that his anger causes him to say things that don't relate to the conflict and only exacerbate the situation. Another person talked about wishing he didn't feel compelled to respond so quickly in conflict situations, knowing that his first response was more likely the one he would later regret. The group plans to return to this discussion later to see how we as individuals and as a group can support the desired behavior changes of our members.

How Can You Benefit from Conflict?

Thus far in this chapter, you have read how conflict is something most people want to avoid, how it sometimes shuts down good discussion, that it can be disruptive of small group life, and that some people would like to handle conflict differently but find changing is difficult. There is even the hint, among some people, that they should not experience conflict because of the way they interpret the biblical admonition to love one another or to turn the other cheek. Thinking about the benefits of conflict is difficult, but a good topic for your small group discussion would be to ask the question, how can conflict be helpful?

Sometimes new solutions to problems come out of conflict. When people discover the path to a goal has been blocked, they may find new routes, new solutions. Conflict tells us (and others) what we really care about. Conflict can bring a group together and unify their efforts (especially if the conflict involves another group). For example, when one nation threatens another, it quickly brings people together in a cohesive fashion. Conflict helps us identify what really matters at our own core of beliefs.

Effectively managed conflicts strengthen groups over time. For example, a family that has over time experienced and worked through several conflicts seems tougher, and when a major conflict appears, the family is more likely to handle it without disruption. The same could probably be said for small groups or for churches. Working through several conflicts enables the group or church to handle the next one that comes along with more ease than does a church or group with no history of conflict.

Conflict will find a way to come out. In a small group, if conflict is unexpressed or unresolved, the long-term effect may be that it erodes the group to the point that the group ceases to exist. If conflict is continually suppressed, then like stew in a pressure cooker, it will find a way and a time to come out. And like that stew, if it comes out all at once, there may be a big mess to clean up.

Numerous strategies for managing conflict can be found in management and self-help books. In addition, if you browse the Web for "managing conflict," you will find hundreds of ideas. My approach to conflict management is to assume at the beginning of a conflict that I do not differ on every point with the other person; therefore, I look for the points of agreement before trying to tackle the disagreement. The question what is it we agree on? begins the conflict discussion. The question what is it we disagree on? follows. Finally I ask, what are we each willing to yield or change in order to bring our disagreements closer together? The heat of conflict frequently will be diminished with this approach as two people find they have more agreement than they thought. Constructive dialogue can move forward much more easily by using the points of agreement than by having to resolve the points of disagreement. I also need to remember the mantra of one member of our small group who, when talking about his approach to conflict, said, "I always grant the other person good intentions."

Remember, experiencing conflict says that you are normal. When your small group experiences conflict, it means it is alive. When you and your small group put the conflict in the open and manage to work with it while maintaining the cohesiveness of your small group, then you have reached a stage of group maturity for which to give thanks.

Quit Talking about It and Decide!

Small groups are not charged to make decisions for the chuch. That is the domain of the committees, boards, and task groups essential for every congregation. Small groups do make decisions, however. Left unspoken, your distress about how decisions are made can function like unstated conflict—and disrupt the group's goals.

As with most of the topics in this book thus far, decision making is also a topic to which your group can devote several sessions. Your discussion could have three parts: (1) How do I make individual decisions? (2) How do we (partners or co-workers) make decisions? and (3) How does our group make decisions?

One way to get started on this discussion is to ask people about a recent purchase they have made and then have them talk about large-dollar and small-dollar purchases. Do they make decisions differently based on the cost of the item? Do they make decisions quickly or after much deliberation? Who investigates and does comparison shopping before making any purchase? Do people rely on advertising or friend recommendations for purchase ideas? People may want to discuss how purchasing decisions represent the way they make decisions in other aspects of their life.

Partners may have some intense feelings about their joint decision making. When decisions affect children, how are decisions made and who makes them? What happens if the partners can't agree on a decision or if one countermands a decision of the other? As the decision topic moves to larger issues—the purchase of a house, changing jobs, relocating to a different city—do the feelings or actions around decision making change?

Just as some people have effective ways to avoid conflict, group members may have effective methods of avoiding decision making. What happens to them in their relationships or in the small group if they avoid decision making? The "whatever-you-decide" person or the "I-don't-care" person thrusts the decision making on another. If the outcome of a decision isn't satisfactory, they don't have to be responsible and can easily blame the other for their unhappiness. If a person really doesn't care about the outcome of a decision and says so—"You go ahead and decide; I don't care," she should honor that statement. In essence, she has decided to give her decision power to another individual.

Once the group has had sufficient discussion of decision making—ease or difficulty, the emotion connected with decisions, and the like—they can move on to examine how the group makes decisions and the effect of those decisions on the group. How does the group decide what to do in its meetings? Choose a recent decision the group has made. Did all members really think they had made their wishes known, and was the final decision one that was acceptable to all?

This discussion may produce a statement from one or more members who will admit that, in retrospect, a decision was not one they liked but they did not speak up to object. If the trust level is sufficient, they may be able to explain why they were silent.

A discussion of decision making will probably produce a different approach to the next decision your group needs to make. Someone will likely call attention to the fact that a decision is imminent and will seek out dissenting or quiet opinions before going forward. Someone will probably ask if everyone has had input before closing the decision. It could become a comfortable procedure for all.

Next Steps

You now have the basics required to initiate a small group ministries program in your church. You have read that conflict and decision making are normal parts of every group—even though we frequently avoid the first and often don't do the second very well. You have read about the things that can go wrong in groups and about some of the issues or procedures that you need to attend to if your small group program is going to get off the ground. And you have read about the skills required to be a group leader as well as the skills required to be a good group member.

I have shared with you, through these pages, a small bit of what goes on in a group. There are people who spend a lifetime studying small groups—and they are often surprised at what takes place in this most natural of human organizations. One of the most accurate statements we can make about groups is that we can't predict what is going to happen in a group. We do know that a gathering of people who exchange ideas and thoughts and who find ways to be concerned for each other enriches our lives in many ways. It becomes a place to share our burdens—and shared burdens are lighter than those carried alone.

Above all, I extend good wishes as you launch your small group program. Whether it is a massive effort that places every person in the congregation in a gathering for a trial period or an independent gathering of friends who wish to go beyond the quick greetings that characterize so much of our lives, I wish you well.

Afterword

◎ Twenty-four Feet in a Circle

You already know a bit about the 12 people with whom I have gathered every Wednesday evening for the past 16 years. The group has been so important to me that I would like to share more of our journey with you.

My small group ends its weekly Wednesday evening sessions with prayer. Sometimes, as we stand in a circle with our arms around each other, someone will comment, "Look! There are 24 feet in the circle." Twenty-four feet: that means all 12 of us are present. Such gatherings are rare, given the busy travel, work, and volunteer schedules we all maintain. They are also precious, because our time together over the past 16 years has become a key part of life to each one of us.

Bits and pieces of what we have done since our beginning have made their way into this book in the form of illustrations, guidelines, and stories. We began meeting when Bill, Ellen, Jim, and Janet invited us to participate in six sessions of a *koinonia* group using a 1977 mimeographed guide prepared by a task force from the First Presbyterian Church in Bethlehem, Pennsylvania. The six sessions have extended to 16 years.

When we began meeting, 10 of the 12 people were relatively new to the community and away from extended families. Ten of the original 12 remain in the group today. Nine other people have joined us as vacancies occurred. Seven of them then moved on for various reasons. The two newest members joined the group nearly eight years ago at a time when they had decided to seek jobs elsewhere because they hadn't connected to any group or organization and felt estranged in this new community. At present, we may be on the brink of losing them, as they now telecommute to work much of the time and spend more time away in a second home in Colorado. We maintain contact with former members and have attended some of their celebrations—weddings and the like—when it has been convenient to do so.

Shortly after we decided to extend beyond the six-session trial period, the seven-year-old daughter of one couple was diagnosed with a difficult childhood cancer. Her parents leaned on members of the group for comfort through the treatment years, and we offered many prayers of support. The group became a place where it was OK to cry out about the injustice of seeing a child suffer, a place where it was OK to question our understanding of God. We now celebrate the medical checkups that signal remission and look forward to hugs from the college junior in her pursuit of a medical career. Recently she worked as a counselor for a children's cancer camp where she was once a camper. We are proud of her ability to say the right thing to the young children there who discovered that some of the friends from the previous year hadn't made it and wouldn't return.

We have watched the children of members go through the struggles that most children endure through grade school, junior high, high school, and college. In 16 years, our children have changed. And we take delight in seeing some of them, adults now, organizing their own small groups for conversation, study, and mutual support, knowing they have said they recognize what the small group has meant for their parents and want something like that for themselves.

In 16 years most of us have had our own medical issues to deal with. Whether they involved a minor "procedure" or extensive surgery, we knew we could count on hospital visits from members of the group. We have talked about why men approach discussion of prostate surgery through humor, and we have talked about how surgery and hospital gowns take away some of the privacy from our lives. Several of us have had the same nurse in the short-term treatment center who always seems to say, "Oh, I'm sorry" as she makes the second attempt to insert the IV needle.

Family members and friends have died during our group's time together. Nine of our parents plus a sister and two cousins have died in the past 16 years. The deaths have prompted long discussions about parents and what we see time and illness doing to the once-strong central figures in our lives. We have worked together to help move a parent from an apartment to an independent living center, then later to an assisted living center, and later still to an Alzheimer's unit. Death and a memorial service followed. The deaths have led to us talking about ourselves and the changing conditions we know will be in our future. We have discussed living wills and instructions about end-of-life decisions.

Many of our discussions—our "lessons"—have focused on families of origin and lessons we learned as children. Nearly every time we begin discussion of a topic—the meaning of money, situational ethics, problem solving, honesty, religious beliefs, politics, manners, appropriate dress or social custom—at some point, someone will ask, "What did you learn about that as a child?" or "Who influenced you about those issues when you were a child?" or "What did your parents think about those issues?" Those discussions frequently slide into speculation about what our own children will think and say and do when they are the age we are today.

Some of our discussions have turned into adventures. On Bill's 10th birthday, his father was killed when his private plane crashed into a mountain top in northwest Nevada while flying home for Bill's birthday celebration. Fifty years later, four of us made a nine-hour drive, slept in a smoke-filled truck stop motel, then climbed the peak to scramble through rocks and brambles in search of some small piece of that plane. The quest failed to find any pieces of wreckage, but it brought a small degree of closure to a man robbed of a father's presence in his young life. Now, new information and better maps suggest the search area was a little off, so a return trip is in the offing. Surely some fragment of that plane remains—and in that fragment, an additional degree of closure may be found.

The group has been a source of support for individuals throughout our years together. Joan talks about a time when she was struggling with deep depression and two members of the group came to the house, pounded on the door, and yelled that they weren't leaving until she let them in to talk. Because of that assertive move on the part of Ellen and Janet, Joan took a step into the open, and that led to discussions in the group on depression, our mental states, up and down times in our families, and sources of support. The test of our helping relationship we decided was, "Who could you call at 3:00 AM if you needed to talk to someone?" The late-night call has been tested on several occasions. Jim M. (we once had three Jims in the group—only two now) talks about a 5:00 AM call for road assistance from 50 miles away and still praises Bill's quick response. There have been some hasty phone calls to take people to emergency rooms or to get kids from school because someone was delayed. We call for assistance more frequently during the day to move items, lift and load, or provide the second set of hands when needed. In nearly every instance, some discussion follows at our next small group gathering about giving and receiving help. We agree that it is easier to give help than to ask for help.

On Wednesday nights we have discussed the ups and downs of businesses and jobs. As Doug says, "The group is a place where I can have conversations I wouldn't have at work." Members have used the group as a place to unload the stress surrounding business, personal, financial, or other issues, knowing that it is a confidential forum of respected friends.

The 12 members of the group have individual passions and causes. The group has encouraged those causes, been involved in some of them, and provided a place where the joys and frustrations of those efforts are discussed. We enjoy stories of Rick's annual pilgrimages to another Civil War battlefield and celebrate his reaching Life Master status as a bridge player. Joan's work with persons of many races and her efforts to eliminate racism have been the topic of many Wednesday night discussions. One evening, the group drove to the nearby state prison to participate with Joan in a meeting of the Black Men's Culture Organization—Uhuru Sa Sa. The experience created several conversations about how we felt when the steel gates slammed shut behind us as we made our way through the different levels of security checks.

Debbie and Linda both put their needles to work to make quilts and fleece garments. Sewing provides a great way to shift energies and stress away from working with preschoolers (Debbie) or statistical reports (Linda). Linda is developing a business project from her sewing and Debbie presides at a quilt group that contributes their efforts to needy folks. We frequently get to see finished projects at Wednesday night gatherings.

Jim M.'s trips to Guatemala have enabled us to help meet the health needs of Guatemalan people by purchasing vitamins and over-the-counter drugs to fill his suitcase. The group continues to encourage his passionate conviction to help people in dire need and even to chuckle at his story of buying school supplies for 42 children in a local low-income support program. Juggling different schools, different grades, and different lists of needed supplies almost did him in. His experience in Central America has also prompted discussions of church budgets and expenditures: how can we complain about a church budget of more than a half million dollars when a fraction of the amount would work miracles among the undernourished children we see in the pictures Jim brings back? To watch his enthusiasm and energy related to those trips—and how it differs from the stress of running a business—creates more discussion. How do we give voice to and act on our passions?

Over the years, we have gone on a number of retreats—at least that's what we have called them, for lack of a better name. They usually start with a suggestion from Joyce that turns in to a scramble to find a common date—nearly impossible for the 12 of us. We have escaped to the mountains in winter, a metropolitan B&B in the heat of August, the coast in the damp fall weather, and points in-between.

Our retreats are usually a combination of rest, food, shopping (we have champion shoppers in our group), and some serious discussion. We use the retreat times to raise questions about how we are functioning as a group, whether we have drifted away from our goals, and what social-service project we might undertake. We also talk about whether we should be doing something different with our lives. Usually our retreats end with a closing ritual or ceremony, and we depart with pebbles in our pockets, strings on our wrists, or written notes of appreciation. A retreat can't end without taking photos. Our collection of pictures stretches over time, different hairstyles, and different hair colors. They are memorable.

Other annual events have become marker celebrations for us. Shortly after we began as a group, we decided to attend the Ash Wednesday service together in place of our regular meeting in a home. The 12 of us boosted the evening attendance by quite a bit, and because the service was over more quickly than our usual discussion, we wore our ashes en masse as we moved to the Dairy Queen for ice cream and discussion. Thus began the annual "DQ session" to begin Lent. We also gather atop a coastal mountain on the first Saturday in August for breakfast, which Joan and I cook over charcoal and camp stove. Guests—clergy and friends—are invited for that one, and the gathering often includes our children. This year 28 stood in the invocation circle looking over the fog-shrouded valley below—then enjoyed the traditional scrambled eggs, corned-beef hash, and Joan's biscuits cooked in a charcoal oven.

During Christmas we sometimes need a room at church in order to bring all our returning family members together for checking in and conversation and to share soup, bread, and cookies. Being away from extended families prompts shared meals during holidays for those who don't have other family members in town.

Three members' children have been married in recent years, and we all attended Janet and Jim S.'s daughter's wedding in Washington, D.C. The photo from that event shows us in our finest—as does the group photo when we volunteered to chaperone Bill and Ellen's daughter's high school prom. We are now at the stage where new grandchild pictures have high priority on Wednesday nights.

Our work projects have brought us together almost as much as some of the health or other struggles we have shared. Whether we were painting a classroom at church; cleaning up a family's house; cleaning the apartment of an elderly parishioner moving to assisted living; sorting donated clothes at the social service agency where Janet, Jim S., and Jim M. have all been board members; or building a porch railing on a low-income house, we gained a great deal by working together. We have also learned through those ventures. We learned that if Jim S. gets a chainsaw in his hands, little will be left of the tree he prunes. That gave rise to the group's expression, "trimming trees," which always draws a chuckle—it means going to the extreme on what you do.

The discussions following our work projects have been valuable. We have talked about our current status in life, what life was like when we were children growing up, what money and possessions really mean, and what it is like to be able to help another. Sometimes our Wednesday night is spent in reading and talking about a Bible passage—frequently accompanied by a careful study someone has done after using Google to browse the references.

All of the discussion questions included as "Session Topics to Explore" included in appendix A of this book have been used in one form or another as part of our Wednesday night sessions. Whether we have talked about difficult decisions we have made, how we met our spouses, embarrassing moments, nicknames, lessons learned from our parents, anger, or changes we have had to make, the discussions are rich and we work to listen to each other and understand.

We have studied books. We recently read Marcus Borg's *The Heart of Christianity* and attended one of his lectures. It took us months to get through all the discussion. Doug has led us through sessions on the Myers–Briggs Type Indicator and tried to explain chaos theory to us. Lessons may begin with a clipping from the news that forces us to think, or a couple may present a challenging question they worked on during their morning walk. In all of this, we continue to talk, we continue to learn about each other, and we continue to learn about ourselves.

Our immediate and extended families are different from the way they looked 16 years ago. We don't look as European as we once did and, while most of us are empty nesters, Jim and Joyce added two young children from Samoa to their family. Adult children have moved away; Joan and I delight in a grandchild who was born in China, and Bill and Ellen have to fly to Japan to see their two grandchildren. They bring back delightful stories of Japanese-American, bilingual children living in a world very different from ours.

As for me, it has been wonderful to have a place where I can be Brooke and not have to be the teacher or leader except when it's my turn. Sixteen years ago, I didn't want to join anything—especially a bunch of strangers who said they wanted to meet every week. With great reluctance, I agreed to participate for six weeks as a concession to my spouse, who needed a place to connect in a new community. I now look forward to Wednesday nights to see what new thing has taken place, to tell about something in my life, to learn about an idea, or just to enjoy being with a group of friends.

We don't play as much as we say we probably should. Perhaps that is in our future. My wish is that you will find a small group where you can be yourself, where you can explore life issues, where you can have the support of friends in those difficult moments we all experience, where you can reach out to your congregation and community in a way that connects you with the world. It's good to have a place where we can know others and be known.

Appendix A

◉ Session Topics to Explore

Exploring Personal Identity

Beginning Groups

1. Introduce yourself to the group and include three characteristics about yourself.
2. Select one to three items from your billfold or purse and talk about what those items mean to or for you.
3. Name one or two positive experiences from your early years in school. What made them so positive?

Experienced Groups

1. Talk about a nickname (or names) you have been called and how you feel about the names.
2. Talk about something from your past that you have lost, and explain its meaning and significance for you.
3. Name one or two painful experiences from your early years in school. What made them so painful?

Mature Groups

1. What name would you be called if you were to start over today? Where does the new name come from?

2. What is something you have never had or asked for that would change your life today (exclude money from your answers)?
3. Talk about a time when you caused pain for another person. How do you feel about that today?

Exploring Church Relationships

Beginning Groups

1. What was your church experience like as a child? If you didn't go, why not?
2. Talk about some Sunday school experiences you had as a child.
3. What was the best thing about church as a youth?

Experienced Groups

1. What do you remember about first joining a church?
2. Can you name a value or lesson that you hold today that came from a Sunday school or church experience as a child?
3. What do you like best about church? What is most difficult about church?

Mature Groups

1. When have you questioned the value of your church membership? Why?
2. What have been your greatest concerns about Sunday school or church?
3. How has church shaped the person you are?

Exploring Spirituality

Beginning Groups

1. As a child, what image of God did you have? What shaped that image?
2. What kinds of prayers did you hear as a small child? Who prayed them?

Experienced Groups

1. When did you question the existence or nature of God and how did that come about?
2. When did you begin to pray on your own? What did you pray about?

Mature Groups

1. How do you envision God? What presently challenges that vision?
2. When is prayer most helpful to you, and when are you most discouraged with prayer? Why?

General Discussion Topics

Beginning Groups

1. Describe a change you have experienced.
2. Who were your early heroes? What made them heroes?
3. What are some of the things you enjoy doing?
4. What did you enjoy doing as a child?
5. What was it like to be a (boy or girl) when you were a child?

Experienced Groups

1. Describe a change you have made in the past five years.
2. Who is someone who was once a hero but is no longer a hero for you?
3. What was your first experience with death?
4. What was it like to be a (boy or girl) when you were a child?
5. When did you develop a sense of what it means to be a (man or woman)?

Mature Groups

1. Describe a change you made that you resisted making. Why did you resist, and why did you make it?
2. How are you a hero or model to other people?
3. What do you envision about your own death?
4. What would you enjoy doing that you aren't doing now? What prevents you from doing that?
5. What expectations do you think others have of you because you are a (man or woman)? How do you deal with those expectations?

Appendix B

◎ Warming Up: Discussion Starters for Small Groups

Prepare one set of questions for each small group, each question on a card. (I print the questions on mailing labels and then stick them to file cards—an easy way to create duplicate sets of cards for multiple groups.) Each person in the group can draw a card and respond to the question. As in most small group exercises, people should be able to "pass" or to reject the card if they choose. When the person finishes his or her answer, the next person can either (a) respond to the same question or (b) draw a new card

While one person answers, others in the group practice listening skills—giving the speaker their attention and avoiding interrupting with either questions or their own story. You are encouraged to make up your own questions to add to the sets below. More experienced groups can be given more difficult questions ("difficult" meaning more personal or more controversial).

Sample questions are presented here for groups of youth and adults. One variation on the exercise is to use a stopwatch and allow 60 seconds for each response. (Some people will find that too long and others too short.)

Following a recent church potluck dinner, I used the questions with 28 adults who were seated at round tables in groups of six, and the questions seemed to be so effective that it was difficult to get them to stop talking.

Younger Group

- Who was your favorite teacher in grade school? Why?
- How did you meet your best friend?
- What job or career would you like to have?
- Who is someone you admire?
- What is your most embarrassing moment?
- What is an example of a hard decision you have had to make? What made it hard?
- Do you have a nickname? How did you get it? Do you like it?
- What is an important lesson you learned from your father?
- What is an important lesson you learned from your mother?
- Who gives you encouragement?
- What makes you angry? How do your friends know that you are angry?
- What is the hardest thing about being a young person?
- What do you like best about church?
- Who decided you should attend the church you go to?
- If you could change one thing about your church, what would it be?
- When you think about yourself in the future, what do you see yourself doing? Where will you be?
- Who is your favorite relative?
- What was a time when you were afraid?
- Talk about an experience you have had with someone of a different culture. What did you learn about yourself?
- Make up your own question.
- What is something about you that you don't think anyone in the group knows?

Older Group

- What is an example of a hard decision you have had to make? What made it hard?

- Who was your favorite teacher? Why?
- How did you meet your spouse or partner?
- How did you meet your best friend?
- What was the first job you ever had?
- Who is your favorite relative? Why?
- Who is the most unforgettable character you have met?
- What is your most embarrassing moment?
- When growing up, did you have a nickname? Did you like it?
- What is an important lesson you learned from your father?
- What is an important lesson you learned from your mother?
- What was the most important (or difficult) career or life decision you ever had to make?
- What makes you angry? How do you show it?
- What was the hardest thing about raising children?
- What do you like best about the church?
- Why did you become a [insert denomination]?
- If you could change one thing about your church, what would it be?
- What is the hardest thing about being the age you are? Or, if you could do now what you could do at 21, what would that be?
- What is the best thing about being the age you are now?
- What was a time when you were afraid?
- Who gives you encouragement?

Appendix C

◎ Training Small Group Leaders: A Workshop

Activities marked with an asterisk (*) can be completed in a three-hour time block. Add other activities to fit the available time.

*Get Acquainted

Objective

To get acquainted

Time Required

15 minutes

Activity

1. Have participants make name tags.
2. Inform participants about facilities and distribute copies of agenda for the workshop.
3. Instruct participants to sit in circles with a maximum of six people, chairs close for conversation (try to not have people at tables).

4. Have participants introduce themselves in the group with their name and one idea or thought they have about leadership.

*Listening and Speaking 1

Objectives

To learn about others through the speaking and listening exercise
To discuss listening and speaking dynamics

Time Required

30 minutes

Activity

1. Place discussion starter cards from appendix B facedown on the floor or on a chair in the middle of the circle. Tell participants that each person will draw a card and have 60 seconds to respond to the question. Other group members should listen and may not interrupt or ask questions of the speaker. Use six minutes to complete one cycle of talking-listening.
2. Ask each small group to discuss:

   a. What was it like to talk for one minute without interruption?
   b. What was it like to listen for one minute without being able to ask questions or comment?
   c. Which was easier to do—talk or listen?

Post comments from the groups on newsprint.

Listening and Speaking 2

Objective

To experience additional listening and speaking

Time Required

45 minutes or less

Activity

1. Explain open- and closed-ended questions: An open question can't be answered with a yes or a no. A closed question can be answered with a yes or a no.
2. Ask participants to complete a second round of responses to the discussion card questions. This time (a) each group member may talk as long as he or she likes; (b) others in the group may ask open-ended questions. (You will need to stop the activity in 30 minutes to debrief, so not all members may have a chance to talk.)
3. To debrief, ask participants:

   a. What was it like to talk without time limits?
   b. How did the opportunity to ask questions change what happened for the speaker and for the listener(s)?
   c. What did you learn about yourself as a listener and as a speaker?
   d. If you didn't have a chance to talk, what was that like for you?

Group Experience Survey

Objective

To assess group experiences

Time Required

20 minutes

Activity

Invite participants in their small groups to identify the different small group experiences they have had. Each person briefly describes one experience, then the next, and so on through several rounds.

Note: Some people may not wish to name groups they have been in if the group involves something they don't wish to reveal—such as an AA group or mental health support group. Assure participants that no one is forced to name experiences if they don't wish to.

*Group Experience Assessment

Objective

To assess group experiences

Time Required

30 minutes

Activity

1. Participants take turns identifying good and bad experiences from groups they have been in, which will affect their own leadership. Ask participants to describe specific behavior or activities—for example, "The leader made certain people had sufficient time without cutting people off" and "One person dominated every conversation."

2. Large group debriefing. Ask the group, "What makes a group experience good or bad for you?"

*Leader Skill Inventory

Objectives

To describe a leader's own leadership strengths and concerns

To create an agenda for additional training

Time Required

35 minutes

Activity

1. Ask participants to think about the good and bad group experiences they have had and to write a personal list of what they think they are comfortable and uncomfortable doing as a potential group leader. Strengths are the things they are comfortable doing as a group leader. Concerns are those things they are uncertain of or uncomfortable with as a potential group leader. The lists may include situations they feel they would or would not like to have happen in a group.
2. In small groups, ask participants to contribute strengths and concerns from their personal lists and record the strengths and concerns in two columns on newsprint.
3. In the small groups, discuss what strengths and concerns group members have in common.
4. Ask each group to identify the most critical concerns on their lists and post those for the total group.
5. Explain that the lists will be used to set the agenda for subsequent training.

*Leader Characteristics

Objective

To identify leader characteristics

Time Required

30 minutes

Activity

The workshop leader can distribute a list of leader skills from chapter 2, in addition to the list of leader behaviors developed in the small groups. In the large group, describe each of the skills and have participants expand those definitions with their own examples. (Some of this material can be prepared in advance as a handout.)

*Leader Concerns

Objective

To identify concerns about leadership skills

Time Required

20 minutes

Activity

1. Use the list of concerns about leadership that participants previously developed. Add to the list those concerns in the chapter "What to Do About . . . ?"
2. Ask each participant to read through the posted concerns and select two or three he or she believes are

most critical for them to learn to work with as a group leader.

3. Ask participants to pair off with another member of their small group to talk about the concerns they have selected. With their partners, participants discuss the concern or a leader skill they don't feel they possess and how they believe they can acquire or master that skill.

Problems in Groups

Objective

To find ways to work with problems in groups

Time Required

30 minutes

Activity

1. Invite the small groups to make one list of the problems they have encountered or they anticipate in groups. (Note: Structure these activities clearly enough to avoid overlap with the list of concerns developed in the activity above. If there are questions about the task, clarify that the activity "Leader Concerns" is intended to describe leader skills; the objective of this activity, "Problems in Groups," is to describe anticipated problems. Use the list of "Problems in Groups" from chapter 5 to augment the lists that participants make.)

2. In the time available, have participants discuss how, as leaders, they might handle some of the problems identified. (If time is short, the facilitator can briefly present this material rather than having participants generate a list of concerns.)

*Group Role Play

Objective

To practice leadership skills and encounter leadership issues in group situations

Time Required

30 to 60 minutes

Activity

1. Select some of the problem situations from the previous lists and write those on file cards to be given to different role players.
2. Ask for five volunteers to participate in a role play, and ask them to put their chairs in a small circle. (If possible, the role-play group should sit in the center of the room, with the other participants forming a larger circle around them.)
3. Ask for a volunteer to play the role of the leader.
4. Distribute role cards (silent member, topic changer, dominant speaker, or the like) to several people, asking them not to reveal their role except through their behavior.
5. Give the group a topic to get them started—for example, a difficult decision they have had to make. Role players can either use their own or a made-up experience.
6. Tell those who are not in the role play that their task is to be silent observers. What does the leader do? How do the group members respond? Can they project themselves into the leader role?
7. After 10 to 15 minutes, stop the group.

    a. Ask participants to talk about what it was like to play the role they had.

    b. Ask observers to describe what they saw the leader and participants do.

    c. Finally, ask the leader to talk about what it was like to be the leader of the role-play group.

8. Ask all participants and observers what they have learned from the role-play exercise.

If time permits, take a break and repeat the exercise with a different group of participants and a different leader.

*Ending the Workshop

As you close the workshop, aim to give participants a sense of accomplishment and confidence in their ability to be a leader. Also suggest that leaders can continue to seek help, ideas, and suggestions for their work as leaders.

Time Required

15 to 30 minutes

Objective

To wrap up workshop and plan for future

Activity

1. Ask participants to pair off to:

    a. Discuss what they have learned about being a leader of a small group.

    b. Review their own lists of strengths and concerns about group leadership.

    c. Describe the types of continuing support they would want as they function as group leaders.

2. Invite each pair to join with another pair and share their responses to #1.
3. Ask all participants what they intend to carry from the workshop.
4. Help the group choose a regular meeting time to share experiences, develop skills, and support and encourage one another.
5. Close with a prayer or send-off for new leaders.

Appendix D

◎ Group Health Assessments

Individual Checklist

Rate yourself from 1 (always) to 5 (seldom) on each of the following behaviors, attitudes, or activities related to your small group. When you finish, discuss your ratings with your group to evaluate your own "health" as a group member.

_____ I look forward to meetings of my small group.
_____ I can focus on the person who is speaking.
_____ I find the topics of discussion interesting.
_____ I think some people in my group are more interesting than others.
_____ I don't pay attention at times.
_____ I like to contribute to the discussion.
_____ I think my thoughts and ideas aren't very important.
_____ I don't always have something to say.
_____ I have things to say that I don't say.
_____ I think I interrupt other speakers too often.
_____ I feel confused about some of the discussions.
_____ I am comfortable with tears of others when they cry.
_____ I am comfortable crying when something upsets me.
_____ I am willing to lead occasional group discussions.
_____ I talk too much.

_____ I have grown in my understanding of others in my group.

_____ I feel more connected to people in my group.

_____ I can ask others in my group for help when I need it.

Group Health Checklist

Each individual in the group rates each of the statements from 1 (always) to 5 (seldom). When everyone has finished a rating sheet, use your ratings to discuss your group's health. See if there are things you want to change or improve based on the individual or group checklists.

_____ Group meetings start on time.

_____ Members attend regularly.

_____ The group has a clear sense of purpose.

_____ The group is able to make decisions about activities.

_____ Members use good listening skills.

_____ Differences of opinion are accepted without criticism.

_____ Members demonstrate care and concern for each other in the group.

_____ Members demonstrate care and concern for each other outside the group.

_____ Members can bring personal concerns to the group for discussion.

_____ The group can make decisions.

_____ The group is able to deal with conflict.

_____ Humor in the group is constructive and not demeaning.

_____ Speakers are not interrupted.

_____ All members of the group participate in discussions.

_____ The group can handle strong emotion with sensitivity.

_____ The group ends on time.

_____ Members maintain confidences.

_____ Members do their group work in the group.

Task Group Checklist

Rate each of the following items from 1 (seldom) to 5 (always) to develop a picture of how your task group is functioning. If you decide some changes would help your group function, then find a way to bring those up for discussion.

_____ Meetings are scheduled in advance.
_____ An agenda is available before the meeting.
_____ Meetings start on time.
_____ Most members attend.
_____ Latecomers are integrated without disrupting the meeting.
_____ Notes and minutes of previous sessions are distributed before the meeting.
_____ Discussions focus on the business of the meeting.
_____ The group is able to make decisions.
_____ Members come to the meeting informed.
_____ Attention is given to the personal concerns of members.
_____ Tasks are clearly assigned to people with dates and reporting procedures.
_____ The chair facilitates discussion.
_____ The chair facilitates decision making.
_____ The contribution of all members is valued.
_____ Future meeting dates are well known in advance.
_____ Information to be discussed is distributed in advance of meetings.
_____ People are treated fairly and with respect.
_____ Members leave the meeting feeling a sense of accomplishment.
_____ Meetings end on time.